# Trees Grow Lively on Snowy Fields

# Trees Grow Lively on Snowy Fields

Poems from Contempoary China

Dual-Language Edition

Duo Duo     Tang Danhong
Gu Cheng    Tong Wei
Lan Lan      Wang Jiaxin
Li Yongyi     Yang Jian
Mang Ke     Yu Nu
Mo Fei       Zheng Min

*Translated by*
Stephen Haven
Jin Zhong
Li Yongyi
Wang Shouyi

Twelve Winters Press

*Trees Grow Lively on Snowy Fields*
Copyright © 2021 Twelve Winters Press
Preface Copyright © 2021 Stephen Haven

Copyrights of the original poems remain with the poets or their respective representatives. The poems appear here in Mandarin by permission. Copyrights of the translated poems remain with the translators. All rights reserved. No part of this book may be used or reproduced in any manner whatsoever without written permission except in the case of brief quotations embodied in critical articles and reviews.

Published by Twelve Winters Press, a literary publisher.

P. O. Box 414 • Sherman, Illinois 62684-0414 • twelvewinters.com

*Tress Grow Lively on Snowy Fields* was first published by Twelve Winters Press in 2021. It is also available in hardcover and digital editions.

Cover and interior page design by TWP Design.

ISBN
978-1-7331949-1-4

Printed in the United States of America

## Preface

I FIRST MET JIN ZHONG IN BEIJNG, fall of 1990. Jin Zhong was a graduate student at the prestigious Beijing Foreign Studies University, where he had previously studied literature with the Fulbright professor Larry McCaffrey. When I met Jin Zhong, I was in my own Fulbright year teaching literature at the People's University. Some of my graduate students were enthusiastic readers of contemporary poets in Beijing. I asked to be introduced to them and met Jin at a party where poets Wang Jiaxin, Mo Fei, Xi Chuan, and others were drinking beer and taking turns performing for the group by reciting a poem, singing a song, telling a joke or otherwise getting a laugh out of the crowd. Jin Zhong and Xi Chuan were the only people there who spoke English. Jin Zhong and I started meeting together that year to translate poems by Duo Duo, Mo Fei, and Wang Jiaxin, one get-together taking place in Duo Duo's Beijing apartment, where Jin Zhong was living while Duo Duo was in Europe. We met every few weeks or so, through spring 1991, over meals and drinks, working line by line on a group of 17 poems that later appeared in *American Poetry Review*.

My year working with Jin Zhong was the start of *Trees Grow Lively on Snowy Fields*, a collection of collaborative translations that takes its name from a poem by Mo Fei and includes collaborative work with two other poet-translators, Wang Shouyi and Li Yongyi, in translating a total of twelve contemporary Chinese poets. When I first met Wang Shouyi in December 1990, he was Dean of Foreign Languages at Heilongjiang University, in Harbin, China. My work with Li Yongyi started much later. I first met Li Yongyi during 1997-1998, my second Fulbright year teaching in Beijing. He is easily the most talented student I ever taught on either side of the Pacific. In 1997, he was a twenty-two-year-old graduate student in my year-long American poetry course at Beijing Normal University. Word on campus was that Beijing Normal faculty were so impressed with Li Yongyi that they promised him a position in the English Department, once he finished his Ph.D. Li Yongyi taught at Beijing Normal University for many years and then later became Professor of English at Chongqing University, where he translated the entire body of first Catullus' and then Horace's poetry from Latin to Mandarin, complete with commentary. For the 1700+ page volume of Horace translations, Li Yongyi was awarded a 2018 Lu Xun Prize for Literary Translation, one of China's top prizes for literature.

Wang Shouyi spent his own Fulbright year, from 1996-1997, at Ashland University, in Ashland, Ohio, where I was teaching on the English faculty, so *Trees Grow Lively on Snowy Fields* is very much a result of a cultural exchange that took place via the Fulbright Program. (Li Yongyi later had his own Fulbright year as a visiting scholar at the University of Washington.) But that cultural exchange also first began in December 1990, in Harbin, China, Heilongjiang Province, when I met Shouyi, the start of a long, close friendship. When Wang Shouyi was later in Ohio as a Fulbright Scholar during 1996-1997, we spent the entire year working exclusively on poems by Mang Ke and Gu Cheng, both of them central figures in the 1970s and 1980s Misty School of Chinese poetry.

Still later, on Li Yongyi's invitation, I returned to China as a visiting professor in spring 2011, when I taught two poetry courses for six weeks at Chongqing University. By then, though Li Yongyi was not yet 40, he was already established as a vital faculty member in another of China's elite universities. Earlier, Li Yongyi had been editor of an active poetry web-zine and was widely in touch with many poets. In Chongqing during spring 2012, we began work on poems by Lan Lan, Tong Wei, Yang Jian, Zheng Min, Mo Fei, Yu Nu, and Tang Danhong, continuing this work via Skype in the years that followed.

*Trees Grow Lively on Snowy Fields* is the culmination of a thirty-year celebration, a conversation between friends who shared a love and a curiosity for poetry that might reach across cultures and contribute to a dialog between them. While this collection is in no way representative of any poetic school or period of Chinese poetry, it does provide a glimpse into the work of a group of Chinese poets who were writing in the decades following the breakdown of officially sanctioned poetry, which dominated the literary scene in China during the 1950s and 1960s. In completing this work—in choosing poets to translate, with our initial aim being to share our work in American journals—I followed the suggestion of my Chinese collaborators in choosing poets they felt were important voices in contemporary China. Eventually we chose to keep for this collection only poets whose work came through in lively English versions. Below, I include Wang Shouyi's and Li Yongyi's separate accounts of their efforts in bringing this collection of collaborative translations into being. Here are the words that Li Yongyi shared with me about the work we did together from 2011-2016:

> "My collaboration with Stephen started in 2011, but we came to know each other much earlier than that. In 1997, when I was a postgraduate at Beijing Normal University, he taught me American poetry as a Fulbright professor. I still remember our visit to Mo Fei, one of the poets we were to translate more than a decade later, and a bilingual poetry reading at a bar organized by the same poet for Stephen. Our joint effort in 2011 began with my inviting him to come over to Chongqing University where I have been working since 2009. He stayed on campus teaching a poetry course for a month, so during his spare time we often had a chance to chat in his apartment. During one of those conversations, I showed him some of my translations of Mo Fei (Stephen's old friend and a gardener renowned for his meditative, pithy poems) and Yang Jian (an emerging poet with Buddhist inclinations and a radical cultural conservative). Stephen offered to work with me on the drafts, and I learned a great deal in the process. His suggestions of changing a few words or phrases would always bring a perfecting touch to the English versions. These revisions usually were not about

grammar, but had more to do with aesthetic judgment: how to play down the overly sentimental, how to sharpen the focus, how to replace images or expressions that are justified in the Chinese context but sound vague, tepid or lifeless in English.

"After Stephen returned to the States, we carried on our cooperation via Skype. Usually I spent two weeks translating some ten poems of a poet, and then we discussed the drafts online and made changes. We talked for about two hours weekly, and it usually took us four such sessions to complete the revision of one poet, and then we moved on. In the process, I was responsible for the selection of poets and for producing a quite literal English version, while Stephen was devoted to making the final renditions artistically powerful and first-rate English poems on their own. When the translation strayed too far from the original, I tried to rein in a little. But both of us are convinced that in literary translation, a creative betrayal is always preferable to a faithful zombie. Between 2011 and 2014, we translated seven poets in total, namely Mo Fei, Yang Jian, Lan Lan, Tang Danhong, Tong Wei, Zheng Min, and Yu Nu, all of whom have made unique contributions to contemporary Chinese poetry. Lan Lan is an adept observer and painter of everyday life, meticulous in skill; Tang Danhong is more rebellious, an avant-garde feminist artist aiming to shock and subvert; Tong Wei made her mark in the 1980s but still keeps her edge as an imaginative shaper of reality, while her mother, Zheng Min, now 100 years old, has miraculously synchronized her poetics with evolving times; Yu Nu is renowned for his absurdist, minimalist short poems.

"In recent years, as I have been buried in an avalanche of workload translating the poetry of major Roman poets, our collaboration on Chinese poems has come to a halt. But I cherish memories of turning ideograms into letters, revealing a world somewhat strange but also reassuringly familiar to Western readers. Stephen has been very diligent in giving these English incarnations of Chinese poems a chance to speak to a wider audience."

Though I never met Zheng Min, she may be the one common connection among translators in the sample of contemporary Chinese poetry represented in *Trees Grow Lively*, as she was a teacher/mentor to both Jin Zhong and Li Yongyi, and is Wang Shouyi's close friend. As Li Yongyi recognizes above, Zheng Min is also the mother of one of the twelve poets represented in this volume—Tong Wei.

Wang Shouyi shared the following memories of our collaborative work:

"My collaboration with Stephen Haven in translating Chinese Misty poems into English can be traced back to the early 1990s. Stephen Haven came to China to teach American literature at the People's University in Beijing, shortly after the 1989 Tiananmen Square Movement. As a Fulbright Professor he was shared with other universities and he came with his family in winter to visit Heilongjiang University. Harbin was covered with snow and overwhelmed by the piercing wind coming down from Siberia since it was getting close to Christmas. Temperatures were 20 below Celsius and there were snowfields wherever we took him outside the university.

"With the excuse of having a Fulbright Professor from the United States visiting the school, the English Department proposed and received permission from the university administration to have a Christmas party. That was a great gesture at that time since Christmas celebrations were no longer allowed in the year after the 1989 Tiananmen Square Movement. At the Christmas Party, Stephen read a few poems of his own, which impressed me with the genuine quality and style. I was delighted when I thought I found another poet who might make a good partner in translating poems from the Chinese Misty school into English verse. The next day Heilongjiang TV reported this Christmas Eve Party in its morning show and again in its evening program. This was a rare event in the winter of that year. It was even rarer that the show included some clips of an American poet reading his own poems.

"After I published English translations of Tang Dynasty and Song Dynasty poems in collaboration with the American poet John Knoepfle—that collection being published both in the United States (1985) and in China (1989)—I shifted focus to Chinese poets in the Misty School. Misty poetry started to appear in the underground journal *Today* in the late 1970s. The journal was printed on a hand-operated ink-printer in the middle of the Cultural Revolution (roughly 1965-1975), in a suburb of Beijing by a group of young poets who grew out of their teenage years under the strain of that crazy revolution. The poetic aesthetics and power of that experience were still influential many years after the end of the so-called Cultural Revolution, particularly in the voice of those who suffered from torture, illegal punishment, from humiliation, loss of loved ones, loss of hopes, loss of dignity, loss of a sense of a meaningful future.

"In this group of young, highly motivated, risk-taking poets, Gu Cheng and Mang Ke were among the most influential. Their poems fully demonstrate many of the essential characteristics of the Misty School. When they started writing they realized their lives had been ruined by the Cultural Revolution though they were still very young. In those dark years they were young and emotional, but they knew well that they couldn't openly and directly speak in poems about their feelings, their ideas, their wishes, their despairs. They knew if they did their lives would be taken immediately as they had witnessed in the case of so many other people in their own communities. They tried to find a way to convey meaning in their poems more powerfully and at the same time protect themselves from government censure and abuse. Misty School poets began to work in images that are much more broadly symbolic and more difficult to tie down to singular meaning. That Misty School poets were influenced by modern Western poetry extended many decades of cross-cultural influence between American and Chinese poetry, which in an earlier era Ezra Pound emphasized so well."

While Duo Duo, Mang Ke and Gu Cheng were all part of the Misty School, with the exception of Zheng Min most other poets in *Trees Grow Lively* are post-Misty School, publishing a generation or two after Misty School poets first ushered in a break with the government-sanctioned poetry of the 1950s and 1960s. During my time in Chongqing and Beijing in 2011, conversations with some younger poets occasionally involved the question of the relationship between new generations of Chinese poetry and the thousands of years of poetry that predate the 1949 start of the People's Republic of China. One especially interesting conversation took place in the company of Fan Bei, Bai Yue, and Zhou Bin, three younger Chongqing poets (all of them in 2011 in their thirties or forties) to whom Li Yongyi introduced me shortly before I returned to the States. We met in a book store. Here is an account of that meeting, which appeared earlier in an issue of the journal *The Common*:

> The bookstore was as new and modern as any in America—coffee, over-stuffed lounge chairs, hardwood floors, ice cream, pastries, floor-to-ceiling wooden bookshelves. Prices at the coffee bar were through the roof—as high as in America. Outside there was the usual chaos of traffic around the edge of a pedestrian mall. Inside was an oasis: Li Yongyi's favorite reading spot. We could have been in any of the smaller American Barnes and Nobles.
> 
> Fan Bei is a Chinese literature professor at Chongqing University; Zhou Bin teaches at Sichuan International Studies University; Bai Yue works in some position outside academia, so that she could be free, she explained to Li Yongyi, to write whatever she chose. Bai Yue's name means White Moon. She had just published a book of poems with Chongqing University Press and brought copies for the other poets. Despite Bai Yue's beautiful new book, handsomely printed, Fan Bei and Zhou Bin claimed that their generation is no longer interested in book publication. The poetry of the younger generation is entirely web based. China made the transition to cell phones long before they were popular

in the U.S. Maybe in this area China was ahead of us again, embracing more fully the way technology was changing poetry.

I asked Zhou Bin, Bai Yue, and Fan Bei their opinion of Duo Duo's poetry. Zhou Bin did most of the talking. Li Yongyi translated for me. The fellow who ran the coffee bar repeatedly came over, with greater annoyance each time, asking us to keep it down. There were other people reading quietly, sitting at the bar or in other parts of the café. Zhou Bin repeatedly apologized to the coffee guy and then went on talking with as much force and volume as before. All three poets agreed that Duo Duo is the best living poet in China, but Zhou Bin felt strongly that his poetry is not quintessentially Chinese. Zhou Bin claimed that there are three essential branches of Chinese poetry—Daoism, Buddhism, and Confucianism. He argued that in working from a Chinese poetic tradition, contemporary Chinese poets should not worry about the differences between these three poetic branches. They had a common root and were part of the same tree. Zhou Bin asked me what I thought of Bei Dao's poetry. I told him that I once had drinks with Bei Dao and liked him and sensed his poetry in Chinese was far stronger than what I had read in English. In English translation, Duo Duo seemed to me the more engaging poet. Zhou Bin said, yes, that's because you are a Western poet and love Western modernism, and Duo Duo writes like a Western poet. When I arrived back in the States Li Yongyi sent me an email explaining in greater detail Zhou Bin's position that Bei Dao represents more fully than any other poet of his generation the tradition of Chinese poetry. Here is Li Yongyi, paraphrasing Zhou Bin:

"Bei Dao, even in his overtly political works, usually focuses on the emotional experiences and responses of individuals. His realm is the personal, the lyrical, yet it is always haunted by the ghost of some threatening political presence and by a pessimistic sense of some hostile cosmic force, against which the hero, usually a man, fights with dignity enhanced by a knowledge of tragic fate, defending his love, his private world and the purity of his beliefs. So there is a beautiful tension between, and fusion of, the personal and the social, and his language, in its graceful, natural, smooth texture, has more affinities with ancient poems than that of any other contemporary Chinese poet. Bei Dao, in this regard, is like a Du Fu in the 20th century."

Then Li Yongyi added:

"I largely agree with Zhou Bin's judgment on Bei Dao and his description of the core Chinese poetic tradition. To my understanding, classical Chinese poetry is spiritual, not in an other-worldly, religious sense, but in a fusion of the individual, either with history or with nature; essentially it is an awareness and a feeling that an individual's experience is always connected with that of other fellow human beings, other species, even with the whole cosmos."

On the far side of the Pacific, where Pound is more famous than Eliot, I loved the idea that the privacy of poetry might open always to the wider "ghosts" of politics, history, and cosmic force.

I will end with passages from a short essay I originally published in *North American Review* when I was asked to comment on my sense of poetry's place in contemporary Chinese culture, an experience that has come to me only by way of eavesdropping on conversations with Chinese poets, when I have been fortunate enough to be in the company of a bilingual Chinese friend, kind enough to translate for me:

It may be hard for Americans to imagine the pervasive presence of poetry in Chinese culture. Even in the modern era that presence persists, though modern Chinese poetry has had to survive the double onslaught of twentieth century communism and twenty-first century communist-capitalism. When I spent my first Fulbright year in Beijing, in 1990-1991, as a tribute to their foreign guest young children sometimes recited classical Chinese poems for me.

The Chinese love of beauty infiltrates the culture as a whole—an aesthetic sensibility that has filtered down through the influence of thousands of years. Among educated people, poetry in China is still regarded as the highest art because it unifies other art forms. Poetry has musical effects, visual effects, the emotional range of drama, and draws also from religion, history and philosophy. My sense from conversations with cab drivers through the window of my broken Mandarin is that even the Chinese working class has regard for the words "poet" and "poetry." The twin spirits of poetry, bamboo and willows, are often planted together in many urban parks. The poets Li Bai and Du Fu lived for many years in Szechuan Province where bamboo and willows grow.

An assault on poetry took place after 1949 in Mao's reformation of the Chinese language. New generations educated to read only Mao's modern reformed Chinese were largely incapable of understanding classical literature in its original expression. Meanwhile there was the muse's other minor inhibition—the ideological correctness of all public poetry in the bloody, political hubris of the People's Republic's first decades, especially during the Cultural Revolution. Only after Mao's death in 1976, in the midst of the Democracy Wall Movement, poets began to write with reckless disregard for state censorship. A revolution in Chinese poetry took place in 1978 when Bei Dao, Mang Ke, Duo Duo, and other Misty School poets began publishing their oblique, plaintive poems in the journal *Jintian* (*Today*).

In April 2011, I had dinner in Beijing with poets Lan Lan, Duo Duo, and Wang Jiaxin. I asked Duo Duo what modern Chinese poet prior to 1977 made contributions to his generation. "No one," he said. "There is no Chinese poet like Wallace Stevens or Paul Celan." In a beautiful restaurant near the American embassy, with caged song birds and potted trees all around us, Lan Lan's twins, and Wang Jiaxin's wife and son, Duo Duo claimed through the Frost scholar, my old student Liu Ruiying, that modern Western poetry was his literary father, classical Chinese poetry his grandfather. In his complaint against the narrative orientation of much American poetry—that many American poets are satisfied merely "to tell the story"—he affirmed his affinity with the lyrical, non-narrative character of most classical Chinese poetry.

Having collaborated intermittently for thirty years on the translations in *Trees Grow Lively on Snowy Fields*, I can say without exaggeration that the experience of meeting and working with the writers in this collection, either in person or through an attempt to articulate their poems in my own native tongue, has been a life-long conversation that has enriched my understanding of the aesthetic possibilities for poetry. I hope the poems of this collection can speak to English lovers of poetry everywhere, offering a peephole, possibly a window, maybe even a portal into the sensibilities of twelve writers who have made and continue to make important contributions to the life of poetry in China.

Stephen Haven, May 2020<br>Cambridge, Massachusetts

## Contents

Preface by Stephen Haven | v

5 POEMS BY DUO DUO
    It is | 5
    Longevity | 9
    One Story Contains All His Past | 13
    The Window that Loves to Weep | 19
    In England | 21

12 POEMS BY MANG KE
    City | 25
    In the Street | 29
    People Age Even After Death | 33
    Vineyard | 37
    Seashore • Seawind • Ship | 39
    Spring | 43
    You, Dead Day | 45
    After One Night | 47
    Close Your Eyes | 49
    Wind from Water | 51
    To My Wife | 53
    The Situation | 55

9 POEMS BY LAN LAN
    The Gecko | 59
    The World with You | 61
    Let Me Accept This Life | 63
    That's It | 65
    Noon | 67
    Only | 69
    Marriage | 71
    Loss | 73
    The Lily | 75

*Continued*

## 29 Poems by Gu Cheng

The Enemy in Defensive Positions | 79
The Truth of It | 81
Elegy | 83
Sunset | 85
Early Summer | 87
Don't Take a Walk There | 91
Cremation | 93
Banquet | 95
Spring Is Dead | 97
Swimming | 99
The Left Side of the Late Night | 101
Yesterday, a Black Snake | 103
Eyes | 105
The Poet's Tragedy | 107
Grassland | 109
Some Lights | 111
Tale of the Turtle | 113
Walk in the Rain | 117
Near and Far | 119
I'm Always Feeling | 121
Little Lane | 123
Sense | 125
A Young Tree | 127
Once We Played | 129
Image with No Added Color | 131
A Generation | 133
Note to an Old Friend | 135
Faith of the Little Flower | 137
The Return | 139

## 12 Poems by Mo Fei

Orchard | 143
Instant | 145
Facing a Stone | 147
That Stone | 149
Falling Snow | 151
The Man Trapped in the Room | 153

Coins Tossed in All Directions | 155
Silence, Just Dust on the Surface | 157
Where Youth Is Not, You Begin | 159
Trees Grow Lively on Snowy Fields | 161
Booming, Spring Shoves Open the Door | 163
Hidden Grains Glisten in Winter | 165

3 POEMS BY TANG DANHONG
You Might Have Been My Brother | 169
Bent Morning | 171
Fake Smile | 173

5 POEMS BY TONG WEI
Little Puppet | 179
Inheritance | 181
The Wooden Horse | 183
Living This City | 185
Shells | 189

4 POEMS BY WANG JIAXIN
Iron | 193
Train Station | 195
Staircase | 197
Change | 199

A POEM BY LI YONGYI
Destinies | 205

7 POEMS BY YU NU
The Preacher | 215
The Watchman | 217
Circumstance | 219
The Action | 221
Depression | 223
Bottle with Water | 225
The Eyewitness | 227

*Continued*

6 Poems by Zheng Min
    April Dusk | 231
    Stone Statues on the Seafloor | 233
    Modigliani's *Woman with Red Hair* | 235
    Crossing Boston Suburbs in Snow | 237
    Longing, a Lion | 241
    Ghost Path, 1990 | 243

6 Poems by Yang Jian
    Twilight | 247
    A Gift | 249
    This Couple in Silence | 251
    Antiquity | 253
    Dusk | 255
    1967 | 257

Acknowledgments | 259

Biographical Notes on Poets & Translators | 261

# Trees Grow Lively on Snowy Fields

5 Poems by Duo Duo

*Translated by Stephen Haven and Jin Zhong*

**是**

是黎明在天边糟蹋的
一块多好的料子
是黑夜与白昼
互相占有的时刻
是曙光从残缺的金属大墙背后
露出的残废的脸
我爱你
我永不收回去

是炉子倾斜太阳崩溃在山脊
孤独奔向地裂
是风
一个盲人邮差走入地心深处
它绿色的血
抹去了一切声音我信
它带走的字：
我爱你
我永不收回去

是昔日的歌声一串瞪着眼睛的铃铛
是河水的镣铐声
打着小鼓
是你的蓝眼睛两个太阳
从天而降
我爱你
我永不收回去

# It Is

It is    a shock of bright cloth
Along the horizon
Bleached by the rising sun
It is the moment day and night
Possess each other
It is twilight    a crippled face
Revealing itself    breaking the metallic wall of night
    I love you
    I will never take back

It is    a hot tilting stove
The sun collapsing on the ridge
Loneliness rushes toward the abyss
It is the wind
A blind mailman    walks into the earth's depths
Its green blood
The erasure of all voices
My words go with him:
    I love you
    I will never take back

It is the song of the past    a string
Of small bells    their eyes staring
It is the clank of river shackles
Beating little drums
It is your eyes    two blue suns
Descending from the sky
    I love you
    I will never take back

是两把锤子轮流击打
来自同一个梦中的火光
是月亮重如一粒子弹
把我们坐过的船压沉
是睫毛膏永恒地贴住
我爱你
我永不收回去
是失去的一切
肿胀成河流
是火焰火焰是另一条河流
火焰永恒的钩子
钩爪全都向上翘起

It is two hammers    striking in turn
The coals glowing in the same dream
It is the moon    heavy as a bullet
Riddling the water and the boat we sat in
It is mascara    sticking eternally
    I love you
      I will never take back

It is    the loss of all things
Swollen to a river
It is fire
The flames forming another river
The eternal hooks claw upward
It is the exact curve of that ignition
Shattering on star-shaped fingers
Blooming    burning still    It is:
    I love you
      I will never take back

**寿**

重温蜜蜂采蜜季节心头的颤动
听到种子的呼吸然后睁开眼睛
奶牛背上的花斑追逐太阳的影子移动
太阳啊,原是上帝的水果
上帝的手就是盛放水果的金篮
——马儿合上幸福的眼睑
好像鱼群看到了渔夫美丽的脸

刚好就是现在的样子:在今年夏天
一列火车被轧断了腿。火车司机
在田野步行。一只西瓜在田野
大冒蒸汽。地里布满太阳的铁钉
一群母鸡在阳光下卖鸡蛋
月亮的光斑来自天上的打字机
马儿取下面具,完全是骨头做的
而天大亮了。谁知道它等待的是什么
一切议论都停止了——来自
古老乳房和七八草权的教导
睡眠和一些坚硬的食物
马儿粉红色的脑子里:大海涌进窗户
波涛也腐烂了,事物的内脏也投降了
由于没有羞耻的能力
树液细弱的滴落也中断了
大树将把太阳的影子从地里收回
小小的车站依旧摆着昨天的那盘棋

## Longevity

Take the quivering heart in the bee's honey-gathering season
Then the breath of the seeds then the opened eye
The spots on the dairy cow's back drift
Chasing the shadows of the sun
Oh the sun, originally, was the fruit of God
And his hand the gold basket for the fruit
The horse closes his contented eyelids
As if shoals of fish
Caught sight of the fisherman's charming face

Now is what it is: this summer
A train runs over its own legs
The engineer walks in the fields
A watermelon steams heavily
Surrounded by the sun's countless nails
A flock of hens sell eggs in the light
The moon's faculae come typewritten in the sky
The horse takes off his mask, wholly made of bone
But now the dawn—who knows what it was waiting for—
Drowns all talk.

The instructions come from the ancient breasts
And the seven pitchforks
From sleep and some hard food
In the pink brain of the horse
The sea surges into the window
Waves rot
The viscera of all things surrender
Because of their incapacity to feel shame
Tree sap trickles to a drip then stops
The tree withdraws its shadow from the field
Yesterday's chess match stalemates in a small station

一粒种子回到记忆深处。宇宙
在猎狐人细长的眼睛里
一只桔子的记忆在他额上流血
而他听到了他们的声音
那是他们正在变成水泥的声音

The sown seed of memory roots
The universe narrows in the foxhunter's eyes
Yesterday's orange bleeds on his forehead
But He has heard their voices
Churning to a wet cement

**一个故事中有他全部的过去**

当他敞开遍身朝向大海的窗户
向一万把钢刀碰响的声音投去
一个故事中有他全部的过去
所有的舌头都向这个声音投去
并且衔回了碰响这个声音的一万把钢刀
于是,所有的日子都挤进一个日子
于是每一年都多了一天

最后一年就翻倒在大橡树下
他的记忆来自一处牛栏,上空有一柱不散的烟
一些着火的儿童正拉着手围着厨刀歌唱
火焰在未熄灭之前
一直都在树上滚动燃烧
火焰,竟残害了他的肺

而他的眼睛是两座敌对的城市的节日
鼻孔是两只巨大的烟斗仰望夜空
女人,在用爱情向他的脸疯狂射击
使他的嘴唇留有一个空隙:
一刻,一列与死亡对开的列车将要通过
使他伸直的双臂间留有一个早晨
正把太阳的头按下去

## ONE STORY CONTAINS ALL HIS PAST

When he opens wide the windows of his body toward the sea
And plunges to the clink of ten thousand knives
One story contains all his past
All the tongues plunge to this sound
And bring with them ten thousand knives
      that clink this sound
All the days crowd in one day
Then every year has one day too many

Last year falls right under the big oak
His memory comes from a cattle pen
A column of smoke rising from it
Some children, burning, sing hand in hand
      around a kitchen knife
Before dying out
The flames leap fiercely in the trees
The flames reaching so far as his scorched lungs

And his eyes are the festivals of two hostile cities
The twin pipes of his nostrils
Smolder with tobacco as they lift to the night
Women fire madly at his face with love
His lips are open for the deep kiss
In a moment, a train blasts past
Running in the opposite direction of death
His outstretched hands contain the morning
His hand pressing down the head of the sun

当星星向寻找毒蛇毒液的大地飞速降临
时间也在钟表的滴嗒声外腐烂
耗子在铜棺的(锈)斑上换牙
菌类在腐败的地衣上跺着脚
蟋蟀的儿子在他身上长久地做针钱
还有邪恶，在一面鼓上撕扯他的脸
他的体内已全部都是死亡的荣耀
全部都是，一个故事中有他全部的过去

一个故事中有他全部的过去
第一次太阳在很近的地方阅读他的双眼
更近的太阳坐到他膝上
一个瘦长的男子正坐在截下的树墩上休息
太阳正在他的指间冒烟
每夜我都手拿望远镜向那里瞄准
直至太阳熄灭的一刻
一个树墩在他坐过的地方休息

比五月的白菜畦还要寂静
他赶的马在清晨走过
死亡，已碎成一堆纯粹的玻璃
太阳已变成一个滚动在送葬人回家路上的雷
而孩子细嫩的脚丫正走上常绿的橄榄枝
而我的头肿大着，像千万只马蹄在击鼓：
与粗大的弯刀相比，死亡只是一粒沙子
所以一个故事中有他全部的过去
于是，一千年也扭过脸来——看

A silenced pistol declares the dawn
More desolate than an empty plate
Bouncing off the floor
Some tree branches snap in the woods
On the funereal street
A fractured pendulum inaudibly keeps
The final time on an old door plank
One story contains all his past
The unnecessary palpitations of death

Fall as the stars fall, speeding toward earth
The earth looks for the snake's venom
So time rots outside its tick tick tock
On the rust stains of his copper coffin
Mice moult their teeth
Fungi stamp their feet on the putrid lichen
The sons of crickets hem his body permanently
And evil tears his face over a drum
Now his body fills with the glory of death
Fills with—one story contains all his past

One story contains all his past
For the first time the sun comes near enough to read his eyes
He rests, a long thin stick on a stump
A closer sun sits in his lap
Another smolders between his fingers
Every night I aim at that one place
With a telescope till the sun dies out
A stump squats where that thin man sat

比五月的白菜畦还要寂静
他赶的马在清晨走过
死亡,已碎成一堆纯粹的玻璃
太阳已变成一个滚动在送葬人回家路上的雷
而孩子细嫩的脚丫正走上常绿的橄榄枝
而我的头肿大着,像千万只马蹄在击鼓:
与粗大的弯刀相比,死亡只是一粒沙子
所以一个故事中有他全部的过去
于是,一千年也扭过脸来——看

More silent than a cabbage bed in May
The horse he drove in the distant past
Trots through the early morning
Death shatters into a heap of glass
The thundering sun leads the veiled procession home
But the children's delicate feet
Step onto the eternal olive twigs
My head pounds, as if a thousand horse hoofs
Beat my drum
Compared with a thick crooked knife
Death's only a grain of sand
So one story contains all his past
And a thousand years turn their faces round—look

**爱好哭泣的窗户**

在最远的一朵云下面说话
在光的磁砖的额头上滑行
在四个季节之外闲着
闲着，寂静
是一面镜子
照我：忘记呀
是一只只迷人的梨
悬着，并且抖动：
"来，是你的"它们说
早春，在四个季节中
撕开了一个口子
"是你的，还给你，原来的
一切全都还给你"说着
说着，从树上吐掉了
四只甜蜜的孩儿
而太阳在一只盆里游着
游着，水流中的鱼群
在撞击我的头……

## The Window That Loves to Weep

Speaking under the farthest cloud
Sliding on the forehead of the magnet of light
Idling outside the four seasons

Silence is a mirror
Reflecting me, forgetfulness

A branch of fat pears
Hanging, quivering:
"Come on, we're yours"

Early spring tears an opening
In the four seasons
"We're yours, we'll return"

So they speak and speak
Spit out
Four sweet seeds from the tree

In the basin the sun swims
The fish in the flowing water
Strike my head . . .

**在英格兰**

当教堂的尖顶与城市的烟囱沉下地平线后
英格兰的天空,比情人的低语声还要阴暗
两个盲人手风琴演奏者,垂首走过

没有农夫,便不会有晚祷
没有墓碑,便不会有朗诵者
两行新栽的苹果树,刺痛我的心

是我的翅膀使我出名,是英格兰
使我到达我被失去的地点
记忆,但不再留下犁沟

耻辱,那是我的地址
整个英格兰,没有一个女人不会亲嘴
整个英格兰,容不下我的骄傲

从指甲缝中隐藏的泥土,我
认出我的祖国——母亲

已被打进一个小包裹,远远寄走……

## In England

When the church spires, the city's chimneys
Sink along the horizon
The English sky's darker than a lover's whisper
Two blind accordion players walk by with drooping heads

No farmer, no Evening Prayer,
No gravestone, no reciting poetry
Two lines of apple saplings, newly planted,
Pierce my heart

My wings make my name known, but it is England
That sends me to the place I've lost
Memory, but no more furrows

Humiliation, that is my address
The whole of England, no woman strange to kiss,
The whole of England cannot hold my pride

In the soil beneath my nails
I recognize my motherland—my mother
Slipped into a small package, mailed this distance

12 Poems by Mang Ke

*Translated by Stephen Haven and Wang Shouyi*

## 城市

1
醒来
是你孤零零的脑袋
夜深了,
风还在街上
象个迷路的孩子
东奔西撞。

2
街
被折磨得
软弱无力地躺着。
而流着唾液的大黑猫
饥饿地哭叫。

3
这城市痛苦得东倒西歪,
在黑暗中显得苍白。

4
沉睡的天,
你的头发被黑夜揉得凌乱。
我被你搅得
彻夜不眠。

5
当天空中
垂下了一缕阳光柔软的头发,
城市
浸透了东方的豪华。

6
人们在互相追逐,
给后代留下颜色。
孩子们从阳光里归来,
给母亲带会爱。

# City

1
Your lonely head wakes up,
The late-night wind in the still street
Dizzy as a lost child
Running here and there.

2
The street tortured like a limp rag.
One big black salivating cat
Calling, calling.

3
The city bitter in its pain
Shaking, twisting
So pale in the dark

4
Sleep soundly, Sky,
Rubbed by the dark night.
Your hair in a mess
Disturbs me into sleeplessness.

5
A ray, a wisp of hair
Falls from the sky.
Oh my Orient, my city,
Luxuriant in the sun.

6
So, People, woo each other,
Give your descendants color.
Kids, straight out of the sun,
Bring love to your mothers.

7
啊，城市
你这东方的孩子。
在母亲干瘪的胸脯上
你寻找着粮食。

8
这多病的孩子对着你出神，
太阳的七弦琴。
你映出得却是她瘦弱的身影。

9
城市啊，
面对着饥饿的孩子睁大的眼睛，
你却如此冰冷，
如此无情。

10
黑夜，
总不愿意把我放过。
它露着绿色的一只眼睛。
可是，
你什么也不对我说。
夜深了，这天空似乎倾斜，
我便安慰我，欢乐吧！
欢乐是人人都会有的！

7
Oh City, oh oriental child
Suckled on the barren breast
Of your grainless mother.

8
Oh zither of the sun, one sick child
Eyes you listlessly.
The only thing to do
Is cast her thin shadow.

9
Oh City, in the eyes of children
You turn a cold shoulder
To their hunger.

10
The night never leaves me alone,
Its one green ghostly eye
Flashes nothing.
The whole sky leans down.
I take what's there for anyone,
What joy,
What consolation I can find.

## 街

我至今不清楚自己准确的年龄大概已活了十几年
可是我却知道我的脑袋什么乌七八糟的事都想
我走在街上双脚使劲儿地踩着一个女孩儿的影子
从我身旁晃悠着走过一个被拍着屁股的婴儿睡着了
离我不远的那个老头儿不知他从地下捡走了什么
谁也不理睬那些孩子们挺着肚皮在大街上撒尿
我突然被吓了一跳竟有人把狗放出家门我急忙躲开
人群中不知是什么人在众目睽睽之下呕吐一地
我视而不见转身发现对面一双大胆而放荡的眼睛
我简直不明白她为何这副模样她为什么要出来丢脸
迎面一个无事可干的男人胖得油亮直眉瞪眼地盯着我
我猜不出他想干什么他肚子里打着什么主意
真是讨厌一只挨了打的猫冲着一个呆子叫个没完
我对着它指手画脚地嚷嚷你怎么不蹿上去抓他的脸
可是这个笨蛋反倒逃跑了我诅咒它决不会有好下场
在高处有扇窗户打开着并且挑出一个丑姑娘的面孔

## In the Street

I can't be sure of my age today:
Maybe I have lived more than ten years.
But I know my mind, my mind
Thinks of filthy things.
Today, on the street,
I step hard on the shadow of a girl.
A baby totters in the gutter,
Then falls asleep, his hip cupped
By someone I don't know.
An old man, not far from me,
Grabs some nastiness from the ground.
I don't know. No one notices.
Kids piss in the street,
Their bellies open to the sun.
Suddenly, a dog of all things
Scampers by. I run too. Nobody knows
Who retched his dinner in the street.
I look away. Suddenly,
A woman, a pair of bedroom eyes
Nails me, balloons like the fat man
Who also stares at me. I hardly know
Why they accost me in this way.
What does that fat man have in mind?
Then someone slaps a cat—
Who knows what for? It runs off
Whimpering to one demented man,
The mad whining to the mad.
I yell: why not jump up and scratch
Someone's face, cat? The idiot gapes.
*O.K., run off! Cat, I wish you*
*No good end.* Then high up
On a building, some girl's ugly mug

我同她打个招呼闹着玩儿却把她的头吓得缩了进去
我真想不出她想的是什么我感到好笑又觉得无聊
忽然一个女人惊惶的声音像急救车一样尖叫着跑过
紧跟着在她后面传来一个凶恶的男人满嘴的脏话
看热闹的人议论纷纷当中还有人比划着下流手势
一个小伙子把痰吐在了那个画在墙上的女人的身上
我差点儿摔了一跤真他妈的居然路上堆着垃圾
那一头碰到我背后的乞丐他双脚在地面仔细的寻找
这会儿看来已经到了晚饭时间只见有钱的走进了饭馆
而一个油头粉面的家伙却急忙解着裤带钻进厕所
街上的人开始渐渐稀少我注意到他们都回家了
就连那个太阳也好像有家似的它这时也匆匆溜走
天黑了下来我仍旧在街上游荡感到肠胃一阵疼痛
我现在真想发疯似的喊叫让满街都响起我的叫声

Pokes out an open window.
I say, *Hey there!*, teasing her
To the point of fear. Such a serious girl!
Then a woman, her face like a siren,
Rushes away. Close behind
The cussing of her man,
All to the lewd amusement of the crowd.
One guy spits, hits the picture
Of a woman on the wall behind him.
I almost fall over a pile of garbage.
*Shit!* Right smack in the road.
Then some bum, so blind he scours
The street with his feet,
Bumps me from behind. In favor of food
The crowd scatters off, the richest
To restaurants. Some sleek-haired guy
Heads for the shitter,
Running, unbuckling on the way.
Even the sun escapes in a hurry
As if it had a home.
Then it's darker. I wander.
In my gut my silence, my desire
The street flush with my mad cries.

## 死后也还会衰老

地里已长出死者的白发
这使我相信,人死后也还会衰老

人死后也还会有恶梦扑在身上
也还会惊醒,睁眼看到

又一个白天从蛋壳里出世
并且很快便开始忙于在地上啄食

也还会听见自己的脚步
听出自己的双腿在欢笑在忧愁

也还会回忆,尽管头脑里空洞洞的
尽管那些心里的人们已经腐烂

也还会歌颂他们,歌颂爱人
用双手稳稳地接住她的脸

然后又把她小心地放进草丛
看着她笨拙地拖出自己性感的躯体

也还会等待,等待阳光
最后象块破草席一样被风卷走

等待日落,它就如同害怕一只猛兽
会撕碎它的肉似的躲开你

## People Age Even After Death

From the bodies of the dead
White hair grows
People age even after death

Nightmares haunt them in the grave
Startle them awake
They open their eyes and see

Another day is hatched
Pecking for food in the fields

Day hears its own footsteps
The laughter, the sorrow
Of its own body, recalls

In its heart, though its brain
Is empty, all the rotting corpses

Day sings of them
And of its own lover
It holds her face steady
With its two hands

Then it puts her back
Cautiously in the grass,
The sexy drag of her body

It may wait for sunshine
But finally, an old straw mattress,
The wind blows it away

Day waits for dusk
When it will hide from you
As if in fear of the savagery
Of a wild beast

等待日落,它就如同害怕一只猛兽
会撕碎它的肉似的躲开你

而夜晚,它却温顺地让你拉进怀里
任随你玩弄,发泄,一声不吭

也还会由于劳累就地躺下,闭目
听着天上群兽在争斗时发出的吼叫

也还会担忧,或许一夜之间
天空的血将全部流到地上

也还会站起来,哀悼一副死去的面孔
可她的眼睛还在注视着你

也还会希望,愿自己永远地活着
愿自己别是一只被他人猎取的动物

被放进火里烤着,被吞食
也还会痛苦,也还会不堪忍受啊

地里已经长出死者的白发
这使我相信:人死后也会衰老

But at night, at night, it is so tender
You can pull it wordless
Into your arms
Play with it as you like

Maybe it will lie down on the spot
Exhausted, its eyes closed
Listening to the roar of the fighting
Of heavenly beasts

Day may worry, on that one night
The heavens might open, blood rain down

It may stand up moaning
At the face of the dead,
A woman whose eyes stare and stare

It may hope, may wish itself
Alive forever, not a hunted animal

Not roasted in the fire
Not swallowed
Though the pain is still unbearable

From the bodies of the dead
White hair grows
Even after death, they age and age

**葡萄园**

一小块葡萄园,
是我发甜的家。

当秋风突然走进哐哐作响的门口,
我的家园都是含着眼泪的葡萄。

那使园子早早暗下来的墙头,
几只鸽子惊慌飞走。

胆怯的孩子把弄脏的小脸
偷偷地藏在房后。

平时总是在这里转悠的狗,
这会儿不知溜到哪里去了。

一群红色的鸡满院子扑腾,
咯咯地叫个不停。

我眼看着葡萄掉在地上,
血在落叶中间流。

这真是个想安宁也不能安宁的日子,
这是在我家失去阳光的时候。

## Vineyard

A small plot, a vineyard,
My own luscious land.

When the autumn wind walks through the door,
*Bam*, *bam*, my whole home
Nothing but grapes heavy with tears.

The yard is darkened by one wall
From which a few pigeons take fright.

The children secret their dirty faces
Behind the house.

The dog that used to hang around here
Runs away somewhere.

A flock of red chickens fluttering
Clucking endlessly.

With my own eyes I see
Grapes falling to the ground,
Blood running in the fallen leaves.

This is the day of no peace.
Who can help desiring it?
This is the day of darkness.

### 海岸·海风·船

海岸

我想把我揉碎
撒在长长的沙滩
我想用我的血肉
去喂饱饥饿的海水

我想让大海的眼睛
深情地望着我
我想让她的睫毛垂下来
掸去颗颗的眼泪

我想把每一次海的喧响
都带到睡梦中去
我想把风暴的欢笑
当成最好的安慰

过来吧,大海
让你沉默的额头
贴上我的胸膛
贴上我的爱

海风

我要吐出
绿色的月亮
它将照耀
我道路的前方

我要举起浪花
向着陆地奔跑
我要亲切地呼唤
扑进她温暖的怀抱

## Seashore • Seawind • Ship

*Seashore*

I tend to grind myself into pieces
Scatter them along the beach
I tend to feed the hungry sea
My own blood, my own flesh

I tend to urge attention, affection
From the deep eye of the sea
Tend to pull down her lashes
Brush away her tears

I tend to bring the sea's uproar
To dream, tend to regard
The laughter of storm
As my supreme comforter

Come over here, vast sea
I'll lay your silent head
Against my chest, my love

*Seawind*

The green moon floating the sea
Spit out of me
It shines brightly on my road

I drive the waves to the shore:
Cordially, I greet her,
Throw myself into her warm arms

告别了
沉睡的海鸥
用手拨开
浮动的海岛

云朵好像是我插上的翅膀
在这无边的夜色里
只有它和我
在一起匆忙地飘

船

在波涛的上面
我竖起胳膊的桅杆
我是被海浪抛起的孩子
遥望着寂静的海岸

只是一片黑暗
只是那合上的眼帘
一只肉体的锚
我把它沉在漆黑的深渊

我的躯体
在海的腹部蠕动
我的泪水
含着苦涩的盐

我的喉管
发出海的呼喊
我的心上
跳动着一片孤独的帆

Farewell, then, to the sleeping gulls
To islands bent under my hand

I put on the wings of clouds
In the boundless night

Only we two
Hurrying off, flocked together

*Ship*

I raise the arm of my mast
Above the waves,
I'm a child thrown into the air
Looking from afar at the silent shore

Nothing but darkness
Not one open eye
An anchor of flesh
Sunk into the void

My body crawls
In the belly of the sea
My tears no less bitter
Than the ocean salt

From my throat
The voice of the sea
On my heart
The dance of a lonely sail

**春天**

太阳把它的血液
输给了垂危的大地
它使大地的躯体里
开始流动阳光
也使那些死者的骨头
长出绿色的枝叶
你听,你听见了吗
那些从死者骨头里伸出的枝叶
在把花的酒杯碰得丁当响

这是春天

## Spring

To the comatose earth
The sun gives its blood
Sunshine floats
In the body of that soil
From the bones of the dead
Green branches grow
From the branches
Glass-like flowers
Listen, have you heard
The clink of that raised wine?

This is spring.

**一个死去的白天**

我曾与你在一条路上走
我曾眼睁睁地看着你
最后死于这条路上
我仿佛和你一样感到
大地突然从脚下逃离而去
我觉得我就好象是你
一下掉进粘乎乎的深渊里
尽管我呼喊，我呼喊也没有用
尽管我因痛苦不堪而挣扎
我拼命地挣扎，但也无济于事
于是我便沉默了，被窒息
象你一样没留下一丝痕迹
只是在临死的一瞬间
心里还不由得对前景表示忧虑

## You, Dead Day

Once I walked in this same street with you
Saw you with open eyes
Dead in the street
I felt the same as you did
The earth suddenly pulled
Out from under our feet
As if I were you
In the stickiness of that void
Although I yelled, although I tried
The sorrow of escape—no use
I sank down and down
Couldn't make a noise
Breathless, vanishing like you
Worrying in the last moment
Of the smothered future

**一夜之后**

轻轻地打开门
你让那搂着你
睡了一宿的夜走出去
你看见它的背影很快消失
你开始听到
黎明的车轮
又在街上发出响声
你把窗户推开
你把关了一屋的梦
全都轰到空中
你把昨晚欢乐抖落的羽毛
打扫干净
随后,你对着镜子打量自己
你看见自己的两只眼睛
都独自浮动在自己的眼眶里
那样子简直就象
两条交配之后
便各自游走的鱼……

## After One Night

You lightly opened the door
Let the night, who slept with you, out
You saw its back disappear
Then heard the wheels of dawn
Rumble in the street
Opening the window
You drove out a roomful of dreams
Swept clean all the feathers
Of your hidden happiness
In the mirror your two eyes floating
As if separately in their sockets
As if two fish after their cold sex

**把眼睛闭上**

把眼睛闭上
把自己埋葬
这样你就不会再看到
太阳那朵鲜红的花
是怎样被掐下来
被扔在地上
又是怎样被黑夜
恶狠狠地踩上一脚

把眼睛闭上
把自己埋葬
这样你就会与世隔绝
你就不会再感到悲伤
噢，我们这些人啊
我们无非是这般下场
你是从黑暗中来的
你还将在黑暗中化为乌有

## Close Your Eyes

Close your eyes, bury yourself
Then you will see, never again,
How the red flower, the sun,
Was hatefully cut off
Thrown onto the ground
Trampled by the night

Close your eyes, bury yourself
Then, in your isolation,
Never again this sorrow
Oh, people, bound to this end
Come from darkness
Soon to vanish in darkness

**来自水面上的风**

来自水面上的风
身上有一股男人的气味儿
它湿漉漉地走上岸
那样子好像已精疲力尽
但它还是很快地钻进绿荫
很快地给自己穿好一身衣服
然后，它停在那里回头看
只见刚刚恢复平静的水面
袒露着粉红色的乳房
那乳房是已临近开放的荷花
它这会儿也许是由于过度的兴奋
它还在那里不住地膨胀

## Wind from Water

Wind from water, exhausted, wet,
Walks toward the shore
What a strong-smelling guy!
He quickly makes for the shade
Dresses in its green clothes
Then, looking back, all's calm again
Still he sees the pink breasts
Of lotus buds, opening, opening,
In the moment before the bloom

**爱人**

假如你的躯体
已还原于小小的黄土一堆
那我仍然愿意像当初一样
躺在你隆起的怀里
我愿意变成阳光
并为你制作成皮肤
我愿意与你悄悄地融为一体

假如你的躯体
已变成春天的土地
那我愿意让自己
失去形体融化成水
我愿意让你把我吮吸得干干净净
那样我全部的感情
就会浸透你全部的身体

## To My Wife

If your body finds first
Its little pile of earth
Then I'll be waiting
As in our beginning
To lie on the round mound
Of your breasts
To change into sunshine
Dissolve into your dissolving skin

Even when your body has fully
Turned to the spring earth
I will still be willing
To metamorphose, to melt
Like snow, so that you
Might suck my love down,
So I might drench you

**处境**

当冬天的风雪
手里挥动明晃晃的刀子
在暗中把我围住
也把我所能看到的
这块小小的天地
封得严严实实
使你找不到出口
我就在这时
听到了不知是谁的声音
那声音颤抖着朝我跑来
一头闯进我的怀里
这使我大吃一惊
急忙用手想把它推开
可我摸到的竟是一棵小树
小树啊，你这可怜的小树
我突然把它紧紧搂住
并对他说，你知道吗
我们的处境是一样的
我们同样都已落入严寒
它们那疯狂的围攻中

## The Situation

When winter's wind and snow
Waving their shiny knives
Surround me in the dark
When they cover the little space
I can see, make it
Impossible to find my way

Suddenly I hear a voice
Trembling, it comes toward me
Startles right into me
Then I try, with my two hands
To push it away—
Only a little tree
Oh, tree, come to my arms
Share with me, I'll share with you
The same shiver
The same mad attack

9 Poems by Lan Lan

*Translated by Stephen Haven and Li Yongyi*

**壁虎**

它并不相信谁。
也不比别的事物更坏。

当危险来临
它断掉身体的一部分。

它惊奇于没有疼痛的
遗忘------人类那又一次
新长出的尾巴

## The Gecko

Never trusts anyone.
No worse than other animals.

When danger comes
It snaps off the end of itself.

It is amazed at the painless
Forgetting: sprouts once more
That human tail.

**在有你的世界上**

在有你的世界上活着多好。
在散放着你芦苇香气的大地上
　　呼吸多好

你了解我。阳光流到你的唇旁
当我抬手搭衣服时我想。

神秘的风忽然来了。你需要我。
我看到你微笑时我正对着镜子梳妆。

夜晚。散开的书页和人间的下落
一朵云走过。我抬头望着。
在有你的世界上活着多好。
下雪的黄昏里我默默盯着红红的
　　炉火。

## The World with You

So good to live in a world with you,
Breathe in your fields
The sweetness of your reed.

You know me. Sunlight flows to your lips
When I hang the wash. A mystic wind

Waiting in the wings. You need me.
Doing my hair, your smile in the mirror.

Night falls. Open books, lost worlds.
A passing cloud. I look up.
So good to live in the world with you.
On snowy dusks, my gaze, the orange fire,
  Silence.

**让我接受平庸的生活**

让我接受平庸的生活
接受并爱上它肮脏的街道
它每日的平淡和争吵
让我弯腰时撞见
墙根下的几棵青草
让我领略无奈叹息的美妙

生活就是生活
就是甜苹果曾是的黑色肥料
活着,哭泣和爱——
就是这个——
　　　深深弯下的身躯。

## LET ME ACCEPT THIS LIFE

Let me accept this life
Falling in love with its dirty streets,
Its tasteless days, quarrels.
Let me, bending, grab
Green herbs at the foot of the wall.
Let me find the charmed sigh of dismay.

Life is what it is:
This black soil, once sweet apples,
Living, weeping, loving—
This stooping—
This hunched body.

**现实**

没有白天,没有黑夜
没有善。也没有恶。
一群人在受苦。
仅此而已。

没有这样的词。
这些风吹散的薄纸的灰烬。

一群人在受苦。
就是这些。
永不休耕的土地里
只有一个女人挎着光辉的篮子
默默地播撒种籽。

## That's It

No light, no night.
No good, no evil.
A group of suffering people.
That's all.

No words.
No cinders of thin paper blown by the wind.

A group of people.
Suffering. That's all.
In fields that never lie fallow
A basket full of light, one woman's arm
Sowing seeds in silence.

**正午**

正午的蓝色阳光下
竖起一片槐树小小的阴影

土路上,老牛低头踩着碎步
金黄的夏天从胯间钻入麦丛

小和慢,比快还快
比完整更完整——

蝶翅在苜蓿地中一闪
微风使群山猛烈地晃动

## NOON

In the azure noon sunlight
A small shaded patch of elm

On the dust road an old bull,
Summer plunging gold in the wheat in its loins

Small and slow, quicker than quick,
More complete than complete—

A lightning flutter of butterflies among clover,
Mountains swinging in that tiny wind

**只有**

只有夜晚属于梦想。
只有寂静的林木
槽头反刍的牲口
只有正午蜜蜂嗡嗡的飞舞——

泉水的倾听。火中的凝眸。
只有一个人轻轻脚步的风暴。
粗糙的树干将别离掩入
怀中——

只有风鼓起窗幔……。
只有稿纸静静的水底
沉睡着万物连绵无尽的群山——

## Only

Only the night belongs to dreams,
Only still trees, only cattle
Chewing cud along the trough,
Only the hummed dance of noon bees—

Spring water eavesdropping, fire gazing.
Only the storm of someone's light steps.
The rough trunk, departure hidden
In its bosom—

Only wind balloons the blinds....
Only in the deep waters of this paper
Mountains of sleeping things, endlessly stretching—

**婚姻**

并不是人们说的那样,爱情
需要一个安顿的地方。没有它
在指尖上狂跳的心脏——
爱所能在一个人心中唤起的爱情的
意外——它一直在奔跑

此后,持续一个奇迹:那最平庸的。
但还是爱——男人和女人。
它在失去中得到。
并在失去中维持:

——两张变得相像的脸。

## Marriage

Not as they say: Love
Does need a place of rest. Without it
The heart beating wild on fingertips—
The accident of love quickened by love—
Runs on and on.

The kept miracle: the most banal.
Nonetheless love—between man and woman,
Gained, maintained
By the loss

—Two faces, nearly indistinguishable

**失去**

一块橡皮的失去里有着
孩子令人羡慕的哭泣。

或者,叶子离开枝头。树摇晃着
鞭子的抽打下风抖开痛苦的宽度。

这一切我都不能做。

我的失去里有一双被砍掉的手
从墙壁里突然伸出——

## Loss

In the loss of an eraser
The enviable sob of a child.

Or, leaves off a twig. Trees sway.
Smarting from whips, the wind unfolds its
clothes of pain.

All this is denied me.

In my loss, a pair of chopped hands
Suddenly shoots out from the wall—

**百合**

她昏了过去。

香气托起她的腰
慢慢把她放倒在沉醉里。

一群迷惘的蜜蜂
将它们做梦的刺
伸进花萼温柔的弯曲中。

## The Lilly

She passed out.

Fragrance held her by the waist
Slowly lodged her in indulgence.

A swarm of drunk bees
Dreams its poked stings
Into the folds of the calyx.

29 Poems by Gu Cheng

*Translated by Stephen Haven and Wang Shouyi*

**守敌**

重要的事是逃走

我的马是竹子

竹枝高悬　屋里

跳
阳光蒙蒙的空地

## The Enemy in Defensive Positions

The important thing is to escape

My horse is bamboo

Bamboo branches hanging high in the room

        Jump
The sun-blurred barren land

**实话**

陶瓶说：我价值一千把铁锤
铁锤说：我打碎了一百个陶瓶

匠人说：我做了一千把铁锤
伟人说：我杀了一百个匠人

铁锤说：我还打死了一个伟人
陶瓶说：我现在就装着那伟人的骨灰

## The Truth of It

The flashy urn says:
I'm worth a thousand hammers
The hammer says:
I've broken one hundred urns

The blacksmith says:
I have made one thousand hammers
The great man says:
I have slaughtered one hundred blacksmiths

Then the hammer says back:
I too have killed one great man
The urn says: So what? I've sealed
In me the ash of that great man

**挽歌**

月亮下的小土豆
月亮下的小土豆

走来一只狗
嗅
月亮下的小土豆

## Elegy

A small potato under the moon
A small potato under the moon

Coming up, a dog
Sniff
A small potato under the moon

**夕阳**

曲曲折折的
夕光
躲过楼群
落在地上

细长的姑娘
发卡闪亮
有多少衣裳
半干半湿
还在阴影里
盼望

早熟的小灯
像金橘一样

下班了
车铃在唱
小心
那片磨损的碎砖
刚画出
孩子的想象

## Sunset

The setting sun's twisted light
Drifts through the rise
Of buildings, falls to the ground

Tall slim girl
Shining barrette
How many dresses
Half dry, half wet
Yearn in the shade?

Early ripe little lights
Golden kumquats

The shift ends
The bicycle bell sings:
*Careful*
One bit of worn brick
A child's fresh-drawn image

**初夏**

乌云渐渐稀疏
我跳出月亮的圆窗
跳过一片片
美丽而安静的积水
回到村里

在新鲜的泥土墙上
青草开始生长

每扇木门
都是新的
都像洋槐花那样洁净
窗纸一声不响
像空白的信封

不要相信我
也不要相信别人

把还没睡醒的
相思花
插在一对对门环里
让一切故事的开始
都充满芳馨和惊奇

早晨走近了
快爬到树上去

我脱去草帽
脱去习惯的外鞘
变成一个
淡绿色的知了
是的,我要叫了

公鸡老了
垂下失色的羽毛

## Early Summer

Dark cloud, lighter and lighter
I jump out the round window of the moon
Over the gathered water of the fields
Such beauty, such tranquility
Back to my village

Green sprouts shoot
Fresh-made walls of mud

Each wooden door fresh
Clean as flowers
The window's paper pane
Blank as an envelope

Do not believe me
Do not believe anyone

Flowers pining with love
Tucked in the hard round
Knockers of your door

Let all stories begin
With the scent of surprise

Soon it will be morning
Come on! Climb that tree!

I shed my straw hat
The husk of all custom
Now I am the light-green cicada
Now I am ready to sing

But the rooster's too old
Drab feathers sweep the ground

所有早起的小女孩
都会到田野上去
去采春天留下的
红樱桃
并且微笑

All little girls, those early risers,
Come to the fields
Red cherries left by spring
Gathered with smiles

**不要在那里踱步**

不要在那里踱步

天黑了
一小群星星悄悄散开
包围了巨大的枯树

不要在那里踱步

梦太深了
你没有羽毛
生命量不出死亡的深度

不要在那里踱步

下山吧
人生需要重复
重复是路

不要在那里踱步

告别绝望
告别风中的山谷
哭,是一种幸福

不要在那里踱步

灯光
和麦田边新鲜的花朵
正摇荡着黎明的帷幕

## Don't Take a Walk There

Don't take a walk there

It's getting dark
A small group of stars
Bloom silently
Around a huge dead tree

Don't take a walk there

The dream is too deep
You don't have a feather
Life cannot sound
The depth of death

Don't take a walk there

Come down the mountain
Life needs repetition
Repetition is the way

Don't take a walk there

Farewell to despair
Farewell to the valley full of wind
Crying is a sort of happiness

Don't take a walk there

Then the light
Fresh flowers around the wheat field
Shake the curtain of dawn

**火葬**

苍天哪,为什么这样忧郁
年轻的海停止了呼吸?
一群群火焰跳着舞蹈
是谁在举行神圣的婚礼?
淡色的嘴唇,再不用勉强微笑
垂落的眼睫,也不用阻挡泪滴
即使整个世界都把你欺骗
死亡总还是忠心的伴侣

呵,花哭了,花哭了
雨墓关闭了人生的小戏
在那闪闪发光的天网之后
飘动着新人惨白的纱衣

## CREMATION

Oh heaven, why are you so sad?
The youthful sea stops breathing
Flocks of flames dance
Is there a sacred wedding? For whom?
Pale lips, no need to force a smile
Half-closed eyes, no need to hold back tears
Even if the whole world cheats you
Death is still your loyal spouse

Oh flowers shedding tears, tears
The rain-grave curtains life's little act
Behind the heaven net of the flashing universe
Floats the bride's gown of veils

**答宴**

我端起那杯苦酒
对生活说：不够

在需要心的地方
请放上一块石头

## Banquet

I raise that cup of bitter wine
Telling life: not bitter enough

At the place where we need heart
Please place a single stone

**春天死了**

还有什么要说？
还有什么能说？

春天死了
她没有悔过

沉默的大地上
漂满花朵

## Spring Is Dead

What more is there to say?
What more can be said?

Spring is dead
She never regretted a thing

The silent earth
Full of floating flowers

**泳**

水平线
在我唇边变幻
使我无法说出
自己的语言

## Swimming

The water's horizon
Laps my lips
Drowns my native tongue

**在深夜的左侧**

在深夜的左侧
有一条白色的鱼
鱼被剖开过
内脏已经丢失
它有一只含胶的眼睛
那只眼睛固定了我
它说
在这深潭的下游
水十分湍急
服从魔法的钢铁
总在绝壁上跳舞
它说
所有坚强的石头
都是它的兄弟

## The Left Side of the Late Night

On the left side of the late night
There is a white fish
Gutted
Nothing left inside
One rubbery eye
Fixes me

It says
*What a torrential current*
*Downstream*
*Steel and Iron*
*At the mercy of magic*
*Dance always on the cliff*
It says
*Brothers to me now*
*All the willful rocks*

**昨天,像黑色的蛇**

昨天
像黑色的蛇
盘在角落
它活着
是那样冷
死了,更不会热
它曾在
许多人的心上
缓缓爬过
留下了青苔
涂去了血色

现在
它死了
压在一座
报纸的山下
难以捉摸
无数铅字
像蚂蚁般聚会
讨论着
怎样预防它复活

## Yesterday, a Black Snake

Yesterday's
A black snake
Coiled in the corner
Alive
Cold
Dead
How could it be warm
It once
Crawled slowly over
Many people's hearts
Left moss
Wiped out
Blood color

Now
It's dead
Crushed under
A mountain of newspaper
Barely even there
Numberless inked letters
Meeting like ants
Discussing the prevention
Of resurrection

**眼睛**

打开一顶浅蓝的伞
打开一片晴彻的天

微风吹起一丝微笑
又悄悄汇入泪的海湾

在黄金的沙滩上
安息着远古的悲剧

在深绿的波涌中
停着灵魂的船

## EYES

Open a light blue umbrella
Open a clear piece of sky

Breeze blows up a smile
Dissolves silently into a gulf of tears

On the golden beach
Rests the ancient tragedy

In the dark green waves
Anchors the spirit's vessel

**诗人的悲剧**

诗人说
地球像个苹果

太阳说
我会把它晒红

于是,海枯了
绿野化为飞尘

只有刚出炉的砖瓦
才没感到吃惊

可敬的诗人呢
早就不见了踪影

难道他的诗里
没写过一条果虫?

## The Poet's Tragedy

The poet says
The earth's an apple

The sun says
I burn it red

Then the sea goes dry
Fields once green fly with dust

There's no surprise only for bricks and tiles
Right out of the fire

What about the honored poet
He took off long ago

Isn't there in his poems
The worm that drilled the apple

**草原**

墨色的草原
溶化着
染黑了透明的风
月亮却干干净净

被困惑收拢的
银亮的羊群
一动不动

让我看看你

你的眼睛
在熟悉的夜里
还是那样陌生

## Grassland

Dark grassland
Dissolves
Dyes the crystal wind black
But the moon is clean

Silvery sheep flocked together
Doubt draws them tighter
Not even one quiver

Let me take a look at you

Your eyes in the familiar night
Still that strange

**有些灯火**

有些灯火
是孤独的
在夜里
什么也不说

在夜里
有些灯　是美丽的
它们做梦
照绿了身边的树丛

有些灯火
是快乐的
它知道熄灭以后的日月
她知道她的快乐

## Some Lights

Some lonely lights
At night
They don't say a word

At night some lovely lights
Dream the bush lit green

Some lights burn with the spark
Of days after they are out
She knows her own joy

**水龟出游记**

一只水龟得意地爬出泥沼,
带着它的甲壳,
祖传的城堡。

它不必躲避鳄鱼,
也不必害怕鹰雕,
祖先似乎已把一切危险料到。

它只需背负着,
先人的智慧,家族的自豪,
好像就可以自在逍遥。

于是,它爬上了乡间小道,
去看野花,去访蓬蒿,
不料却碰上一双农夫的大脚。

水龟赶快就……
缩头缩脑,缩手缩脚,
但还没想临阵脱逃。

农夫欣然拾起水龟,
两面瞧瞧,淡淡一笑,
顺便放进了手提的草包。

他把水龟带给了寂寞的孩子,
作为生日礼品,
据说象征着长生不老。

也许象征得过于美妙,
孩子马上就在龟壳边上,
钻了个小小的孔道。

孔道中穿过了一条旧表链,
另一头拴在桌角,
从此水龟再回不了泥沼。

## Tale of the Turtle

A turtle's pleasure's
Carrying out of the bog
The castle it inherited.

No need to be concerned
About hawks, crocodiles—
His ancestors took care of all that.

What he needs is only to carry
the hard wisdom of the species,
his pride, free from worry.

So he crawls up the country path,
Wild flowers, shrubbery.
Suddenly a heavy foot

In a hurry—no escape—
The turtle shrinks
His head, feet, back into himself.

The farmer picks him up, turns
Him over, smiles,
Drops him into his straw bag.

A symbol of longevity, the turtle
Makes a fine birthday gift
For the farmer's lonely child.

Such a good luck charm!
Immediately the child drills
A small hole in the edge of that shell.

The turtle's not going anywhere.
The chain of an old pocket watch,
Slipped through, fixes him to the table.

水龟呀，总默默地躲在壳中，
是气愤？是怨恨？是苦恼？
即使有上帝也难以知道。

但愿水龟不是在咒骂祖先，
没有告诉它这样的诫条：
坚固的城堡也会变成坚固的死牢。

From then on, even God can't tell
What goes on in the green mind
Hidden inside that silent shell.

If he could, would he swear at his ancestors
Who never gave him this lesson?
His safe haven a deadly prison now.

**雨行**

云灰灰的,
再也洗不干净。
我们打开雨伞,
索性涂黑了天空。

在缓缓飘动的夜里,
有一对双星,
似乎没有定轨,
只是时远时近……

## Walk in the Rain

Clouds, gray and gray.
We can never wash them clean.
Why not open our umbrella,
Blacken the total sky.

In the slowly floating night
A pair of stars
No fixed path
Sometimes near, sometimes far . . .

**远与近**

你,
一会儿看我,
一会儿看云;

我觉得,
你看我时很远,
你看云时很近。

## NEAR AND FAR

You,
In a moment look at me,
In a moment look at the clouds;

When you look at me
Nowhere near
When you look at clouds
Nowhere far

**我总觉得**

我总觉得
星星曾生长在一起
像一串绿葡萄
因为天体的转动
滚落到四方

我总觉得
人类曾聚集在一起
像一碟小彩豆
因为陆地的破裂
迸溅到各方

我总觉得
心灵曾依恋在一起
像一窝野蜜蜂
因为生活的风暴
飞散在远方

## I'm Always Feeling

I'm always feeling
Stars once grown together,
Like a bunch of green grapes,
Due to the turning of the universe,
Roll to all corners of the sky

I'm always feeling
People once gathered together,
Like a plate of colorful beans,
Due to the breaking soil,
Scatter to all corners of the Earth

I'm always feeling
Hearts once spun together,
Like bees in a wild hive,
Due to the stormy weather,
Fly to the far corners of the world

**小巷**

小巷
又弯又长

没有门
没有窗

我拿把旧钥匙
敲着厚厚的墙

## Little Lane

A little lane
Twisting and long

No door
No window

I hold an old key
Knocking at the thick wall

**感觉**

天是灰色的
路是灰色的
楼是灰色的
雨是灰色的

在一片死灰之中
走过两个孩子
一个鲜红
一个淡绿

## Sense

The sky is gray
The roads are gray too
The buildings
The rain

In such a dead gray
Two kids pass by
One in bright red
The other in light green

**年轻的树**

雪呀雪呀雪
覆盖了沉睡的原野

无数洁白的辙印
消失在迷蒙的边界

在灰色的夜空前
伫立着一棵年轻的树

它拒绝了幻梦的爱
在思考另一个世界

## A Young Tree

Snow snow snow
Covering the sleeping field

White tire tracks everywhere
Disappear in the blurred horizon

Against the gray night sky
A young tree stands

Thinking about another world
It shakes off any dream of love

**游戏**

那是昨天？前天？
呵，总之是从前
我们用手绢包一粒石子
一下丢进了蓝天------

多么可怕的昏眩
天地开始对转
我们松开发热的手
等待着上帝的严判

但没有雷，没有电
石子悄悄回到地面
那片同去的手绢呢？
挂在老树的顶端

从此，我们再不相见
好像遥远又遥远
只有那颗忠实的石子
还在默想美丽的旅伴

## Once We Played

Was it yesterday? The day before?
Anyway, it was before
We wrapped a stone in a handkerchief
Threw it up into the sky's blue—

What dizziness, the earth and sky
Swinging terribly around each other
We opened hands warmed by one another
Waited our punishment from God

But no thunder, no lightning
The stone silently floating back
What about that handkerchief?
We looked at the top of an old tree

From then on we never met again
Anyway, it was a long time ago
Only the loyalty of a stone
Thinks forever of its lovely partner

**没有着色的意象**

我的土地
像手心一样发烧
我的冬天
在滑动
它在溶化
在微微发粘的恋爱
在变成新鲜的
泡沫和鱼

狗也会出现
会背着身
像躲藏一千年的羞耻
远处是碎砖
近处
是嗅过的城市
淡黄、淡白的水气
被赶进田垅

它会打喷嚏
那就打吧
让饱饱囊囊的田野
鼓起
慢慢挤住天空
打吧
不要在清醒的刺痒中
停止

停止是岩石
是黑墓地上
那个扭住的小兽
停止
水鸟像大雪一样
飘落下来
夜晚前的丁香树
哆哆嗦嗦

### Image with No Added Color

My land
Runs in fever like a palm
My winter
Slides
Melts
A slightly sticky love
Fresh foam and fish

A dog may also appear
May sulk away
From a thousand years of shame
Smell the city close by
Broken bricks in the distance
Yellow stream white stream
Driven into the field's furrows

The dog may sneeze
Let it do it
Let the full fields
Stretch
Slowly catch the sky
It sneezes again
Won't stop
Not even when it's scratching

To stop is to be a rock
To be that little stuck animal
On the black ground of the graveyard
Stop
Gulls flow down
Like a big snow
Lilacs before evening
Quivering

## 一代人

黑夜给了我黑色的眼睛
我却用它寻找光明

## A Generation

The dark night gave me black eyes
I use them to search for light

**赠别**

今天
我和你
要跨过这古老的门槛
不要祝福
不要再见
那些都像表演
最好是沉默
隐藏总不算欺骗
把回想留给未来吧
就像把梦留给夜
泪留给大海
风留给帆

## Note to an Old Friend

Today
You and I
Step over the ancient threshold
No best wishes
Don't say goodbye
Such useless performances
The best thing is silence
It tells no lies
Let's save nostalgia
For the future
Dreams for the night
Tears for the sea
Wind for a ship's taut sails

**小花的信念**

在山石组成的路上
浮起一片小花

它们用金黄的微笑
来回报石块的冷遇

它们相信
最后，石块也会发芽
也会粗糙地微笑
在阳光和树影间
露出善良的牙齿

## The Faith of the Little Flower

On the hill's stone path
Small flowers spread

They repay the coldness of stones
With their golden smiles

Their faith is this:
In the end the stone will sprout too
Flash rough grins
That toothed kindness
Pocked with shade and sun

## 回归

不要睡去，不要
亲爱的，路还很长
不要靠近森林的诱惑
不要失掉希望

请用凉凉的雪水
把地址写在手上
或是靠着我的肩膀
度过朦胧的晨光

撩开透明的暴风雨
我们就会到达家乡
一片圆形的绿地
铺在古塔近旁

我将在那儿
守护你疲倦的梦想
赶开一群群黑夜
只留下铜鼓和太阳

在古塔的另一边
有许多细小的海浪
悄悄爬上沙岸
收集着颤动的音响……

## The Return

Don't fall asleep, don't, my love,
The road is still long
Don't stop near the lure of the forest
Don't lose hope

Please write with slushy water
The address on your lined palm
Or lean into my shoulder
The whole ambiguous dawn

Wipe away the thundering storm flakes
We will soon arrive at our village
A green circle, a lawn,
Stretched out before an ancient pagoda

I will be there
To guard your worn desire
Drive away flocks of nights
Only to keep the bronze drum and sun

On the other side of the pagoda
Small waves quietly gather
Roll, beach
The hush of their pulsed sound

## 12 Poems by Mo Fei

*7 poems translated by Stephen Haven and Li Yongyi*
*5 poems translated by Stephen Haven and Jin Zhong*

**果园**

和秋天有过来往
秋天的果园青红不分
亲手摘下来的果子是香甜的
苦的还在树上

把石头抛向树顶
落下的都是通红的果子
看不见石头
如果尝到了一种怪味
那肯定是吃错了地方

在秋后
会赶上一场雪
来不及拣走的果子
都是那些烂掉的石头

## Orchard

Touched by autumn
The orchard will become red and green
The fruit you pluck with your own hands is delicious
The bitter ones are still in the trees

If you throw a stone into the top of the tree
What falls is the completely red fruit
If your mouth meets an unpleasant taste
Certainly you have bitten the wrong place

After autumn
Snow will arrive
The fruit not collected in time
Will rot and drop like stones

*tr. Stephen Haven and Jin Zhong*

**这一刻**

雪从山顶迅速滑落
马在地上翻滚
灌木在彼此的怀抱中呼喊
这一刻

是记忆中最长的一年
除非祖父回来点灯
没人敢读完
那则命运般闪烁的寓言

## Instant

The snow swiftly slides from the hilltop
The horse rolls on the ground
The shrubs cry in each other's arms
This instant

Is the longest year in memory
Unless the grandfather returns to light the lamp
No one dares finish reading
That fable glittering like fate

*tr. Stephen Haven and Jin Zhong*

**相对一块石头**

相对一块石头
我的沉默无足轻重
一棵树生长
还有一棵树也要生长
纠缠不清的枝条
拨乱了一种思想的叶脉
我要说什么
我不要说什么
这中间
就有一片积雪
向往冬天的人们
拉出一条深远的道路
让银光响亮的马车满载而归

## FACING A STONE

Facing a stone
My silence is nothing
A tree grows
Another tree also wants to grow
The branches entangled together
Have disturbed the leaf-vein of a thought
What I want to say
What I do not want to say
Between them
There is a stretch of thick snow
The people who have fallen in love with winter
Leaving a deep track in the long road
Return on a full horse-cart with silver-white gallops

*tr. Stephen Haven and Jin Zhong*

**石头**

那块石头长满了野草
雪后
那块石头轰动了阳光

那块石头不再跳动
死后
那块石头落在心上

那块石头是无人知道的精灵
雪后
那块石头从中裂开一道峡谷

## That Stone

That stone is overgrown with weeds
After the snow
It stirs the sunlight

That stone no longer beats
After death
It rests on the heart

That stone is an unknown spirit
After the snow
A gorge is formed in it

*tr. Stephen Haven and Jin Zhong*

**落雪**

看到一场雪
我会想起一个人
一个不曾到过这世界的人
她从来没有见过冬天
飘向心灵的雪花
照透了单薄的窗纸
更没有见过化雪时节
湿润的枣树枝
挂着一动不动的风筝
想起一个人
我就会看到另一场雪

一场不会什么都埋没的雪
她在冬日的黄昏里开放
感到一种降临是多么美好的经历
从寒冷的日子里回来
我终于没有认清
一场雪和一个人
结束在什么地方

## Falling Snow

Seeing the falling snow
I think of a person
A person who has never been to this country
She has never seen the winter here
Where the snowflakes flowing to the heart
Shine through the paper in the window
And she has never seen the snow-melting season
Where a still kite hangs on a wet jujube tree
Thinking of another falling snow
A snow which will not bury everything
I see another person:

She blooms in the dusk of that winter day
Her white descent is an experience
When she's lost
She reveals to me a pure territory
And on returning from that white day
I can't distinguish where it all ends:
The falling snow, that person

*tr. Stephen Haven and Jin Zhong*

**固定在房间里的人**

固定在房间里的人
对那张桌子充满恐惧
文字是大大小小的漏洞
他不知道怎样修补

还不如一页白纸活得干净
完全习惯了
他一直挂念墙上的钟表
能停下来就会更准

预感从太阳穴这边乱跳
他什么也听不清
雷雨惊呆了成片的树木
为着一个恶毒的梦

天说亮就亮了
他彻夜翻滚
是一场毫无依据的大火
使得他在书堆上得救

## The Man Trapped in the Room

The man trapped in the room
Weighed down by terror of the desk,
Words, yawning holes big and small
He doesn't know how to fill—

The life of the white page is much cleaner
Utterly resigned to it
Always the drip of the wall-clock's ticks
Stopped, it would be more accurate

Some unnamed fear rocks his head
He can hardly hear anything
Thunder and rain petrify armies of trees
Please a vicious dream

Dawn comes all of a sudden
After his writhing, endless night
A blaze, descending from nowhere
Illuminates his books

*tr. Stephen Haven and Li Yongyi*

**硬币抛向四方**

硬币抛向四方
天空像发过誓一样清澈
你从不幸的意义上认出
那些缀在词后边的东西

更正日期的使者
离开了自己的家
梧桐树厚重的叶子
夸大了一场雨的分量

从熟睡中不断跌落
灌木的末梢一阵雀跃
为黑夜的来临操心
简直就是在替别人逃命

美好的一课被搅乱
你还能记住她
无知的耳朵在两边
一样寂静一样冷漠

## Coins Tossed in All Directions

Coins tossed in all directions
The sky pure as an oath
You note threads of dark fate
Tassels stitched to words

The messenger comes to change dates,
Already sets off from his home,
The heavy leaves, parasols of trees
Overabundant, a downpour

Cascading deep in their dreams
Shrubs frisk like birds
Worrying about the fall of night
Is like running for someone else's life

That meeting with her, sweet,
Interrupted, lingers in
Your memory: The cold naiveté
Silence of an ear

*tr. Stephen Haven and Li Yongyi*

**寂静仅仅是表面上的灰尘**

寂静仅仅是表面上的灰尘
悬铃木在惧怕中摇晃
所有抱到一起的叶子
让人领受无知的衰老

值得赞美的事物
更值得为它哭泣
没有准备的一切没有牵挂
他腾不出自己的房间

藏匿被死亡征用的书目
最后一批果实在忍耐
秋天的碰撞,里外的剥削
他只能应对种种的猜想

来自时间的驳斥声
让我们的头脑四壁空空
在语言的泥淖中呼喊
从此注定他嘶哑的一生

## SILENCE, JUST DUST ON THE SURFACE

Silence, just dust on the surface:
Plane trees shaking with fear
All leaves bound in that embrace
Grant us the secret gift of withering

Things worthy of celebration
Are even more worthy of weeping
Nothing brings no worries yet
He cannot empty his room

To hide books enlisted by death
The last fruit bunch endures
Autumn's impact, within and without
He braves rumors—how can he help it?—

Rising from time's rebukes
The rooms of the brain left empty
Screaming in the word bogs
Wears life down to a husky voice

*tr. Stephen Haven and Li Yongyi*

**就在青春不在的地方你开始**

就在青春不在的地方你开始
写下早春和发了芽的灌木
从远处写到近处
没有谁能够打断你

黄昏和山色一样壮丽的马
萦绕在园丁的日子里
阵阵鸟声驰向天边
记忆中的树篱绵绵不绝

沉睡的人梦里说话
不眠的人独自工作
枝头的花儿开遍了
这里没有意外的结果

往年堆成堆的杂草如此松散
你只要碰了它蛾子便飞来飞去
只要你想起某个人
整个园子就会安静下来

## Where Youth Is Not, You Begin

Where youth is not, you begin,
Writing early spring, rising shrubs,
Weaving far, weaving near,
No one to interrupt

Dusk and horses splendid as landscapes
Circle the days of the gardener
Bird cries sailing to the sky
Endless hedges running in memory

Sleeping, he murmurs in dreams
Vigilant, he toils alone
Every flower blooms
Nothing here surprises you

Weeds, loosely stacked, not as in past years,
Stir up frenzied moths
You suddenly remember someone
The whole garden sinks in silence

*tr. Stephen Haven and Li Yongyi*

**树木在雪地上活跃起来**

树木在雪地上活跃起来
潜伏的敌人变得阴沉
这个冬天毫无保留
生命知道了自己的期限

黑夜仿佛君王一样富有
大雪盖起的宫殿
牢固得就像一片废墟
重温幸福的人多么凄凉

你经历的每一个冬天
对我也不陌生
所有向上攀援的树枝
碰到了让人惊喜的东西

等一场大雪过后
石头减轻了我们的悲痛
马匹牵动林中的光线
树木的空隙容纳整个黎明

# TREES GROW LIVELY ON SNOWY FIELDS

Trees grow lively on snowy fields
Some gray enemy sneaks in
This winter reveals everything
Life comes to know its limit

The night as rich as a king
The palace built of snow
Strong as an expanse of ruins:
How sad to relive past joys

Every winter you go through
Is all the same to me
All reaching branches
Touch some warm surprise

After a heavy snowfall
Rocks soften our sorrow
In the woods, rays turn with the horse's head
Dawn spills in gaps between the trees

*tr. Stephen Haven and Li Yongyi*

**春天隆重的开门声伴随着**

春天隆重的开门声伴随着
大块的浮冰冲向下游
一些人青春永驻
一些人因悔恨而衰老
每棵杨树都在缠绕
经过三十年的道路
满枝的花穗在一夜之间
从窗前哈出冷冷的清香
你看见影子里的积雪
被远处的阳光渐渐收拢
不断下沉的木料
终于坍在屋角上
一排松动的篱笆
仍旧牢不可破
在无人进去的房间里
说什么什么就会来到

## BOOMING, SPRING SHOVES OPEN THE DOOR

Booming, spring shoves open the door,
Blocks of ice wash down the river
While some people stay young
Some regret and grow older
Every poplar winding
Along the thirty-year road,
Branchfuls of flowers, overnight,
Breathe cold sweetness into the window
You see snow, gradually folded
In the shade by distant sunlight
Wood that keeps on rotting
Collapses finally on the gable
Though the fence gate is broken
It still holds against the siege
In the room that no one enters
Something once said comes into being

*tr. Stephen Haven and Li Yongyi*

**藏匿在冬天的粮食闪闪发亮**

藏匿在冬天的粮食闪闪发亮
漆黑的肥料催动树木的根芽
从马厩里冒出的热气多么虚幻
被死亡逼到门口的人泪流满面

田野返青时的家园无比温暖
埋下种子的世界难以平静
伟大的精神经不起突来的春天
这就到了分担一些事物的年龄

我只能听从群鸟逼近的声音
刷新的河岸裸露清澈的卵石
桃花在开放的季节没有人留步
充满内心的骄傲没有人知道

信守诺言的日子你是多么孤单
昆虫的眼睛触怒绿树的枝叶
挂钟的摆顺势而下不可遏止
为停顿的车辆投上无端的阴影

## Hidden Grains Glisten in Winter

Hidden grains glisten in winter
Dark dung quickens roots and buds
How unreal the hot vapor from the stable!
Death pushes a sobbing face against the door

Fields green again, home at its tenderest
Seeds sown, the world can hardly keep calm
Great spirit weighed down by sudden spring
Reaches the years for shouldering things

I have to submit to bird chatter closing in
Bare shores wash clear pebbles
The peach tree in full bloom stops no one
No one knows its hidden pride

Staying true to promises, your lonely days
The green crowns pocked by insect eyes
Inevitable, this pendulum swinging down
Casting shadows on unmoving carts

*tr. Stephen Haven and Li Yongyi*

3 Poems by Tang Danhong

*Translated by Stephen Haven and Li Yongyi*

**你可能是我的兄弟……**

你可能是我的兄弟,特别是当黎明
那飘向上空的高兴的牛奶味
像白色的青春安慰着肺

我却让肺向白色示爱
让肺长出了孔雀的翅膀
因为我幼稚,还因为我狂喜

你可能是我的苹果,特别是当今天
氧气在肉中失去了甜酸味
像光阴流逝中的一团毛

唯有中年的喉结劝说我呼吸
劝说羽翎应该和树根结婚
你以事后的思考看穿了这一切

你可能是我的幻影,特别是当午夜
从我的怀里,露出纸上芭蕾
羞涩的一角,像一朵花要求精确的身份

我怎么知道,这一切是她造成的
她可能是玉兰花,精神分裂的花
她像飘在上空的天使的阴道
谁注目,谁就要受到惩罚

　原谅孔雀大胆的尾巴呼喊吧
饶恕我的肺,刮着白色的狂风
因为我不自由,还因为我紧张

## You Might Have Been My Brother...

You might have been my brother, especially at dawn
Milky vapors rise into the sky
That white adolescence wafting into my lungs

I woo that white air
Let it grow wings of a peacock,
Naïve and overwhelmed with joy

You might have been my apple, especially today,
But the mashed pulp soured
Like a tuft of hair bleached in time

Only the Adam's apple allowed me to breathe
To marry my feathers to your rooted tree
But you saw through all this

You might have been my ghost, especially tonight,
A shy corner of my ballet,
A painting, a flower, asking an exact identity

How could I know she was there all the time,
A magnolia blooming in schizophrenia,
The vulva of an angel roving the sky
Crushing anyone who dared to stare

Forgive the shout of the peacock's tail
Mercy to my lungs blowing white gales,
Always the anxious prisoner

**他们骂弯了清晨一米**

他们骂弯了清晨一米,
我在幼芽的高度抽泣。
这不关太阳的事,朝霞,
照样任裙子烂掉。
他们骂我。

我骂飞了春天。
绝育梦,盛满乳房的冰雪。
这不关他们的事,
他们吸吮着,痛苦地
堕去我腹中的花。

花骂美了现实。
太阳弯曲着清晨打我。
手从太阳的高度打我的破碎。
太阳之手打我的朝霞。
这不关我的事。
幼芽在一米五的夜烂掉。
冰雪隆起我的胸部。
花隆起了他们。
春天恳求我原谅。

这时,我活不下去了,
一边哭,一边嗅,一边蹲下,
任他们摸疼痛的星空。

这不关爱的事。

星空失去其痛,
星空是我吗?

## Bent Morning

Cursing, they bent the morning by one meter.
I sobbed the height of a bud.
Nothing to do with the sun. Glowing clouds
And my skirt rotting just the same.
They swore at me.

Cursing back, I tossed spring flying.
Dreamed of sterilization in the breasts' icy snow.
It had nothing to do with them,
Sucking, painfully,
My womb's nectar siphoned off.

No beauty without the curse of those flowers.
The sun beat me, bent the morning.
The sun's hands reached for my battered brokenness,
The scattered glow of those clouds.
What did it have to do with me?
The night's bud rotted a meter and a half.
Icy snow welled up my breasts.
The flowers lifted them.
Spring asked my forgiveness.

Then, I could endure it no more,
Howling, sniffing, squatting down,
The star-studded sky groping in agony.

Nothing to do with love.

The starred loss of feeling pain,
The sky mirroring me?

**强作笑颜**

必须每天想起重生的光芒
才能忍受烂掉的生存之痛

必须每天把绞痛的心
捧到怜悯的羽翼下：
银色的 光洁的羽翼 我在烂掉！

必须把夜晚想成夏夜
把夏夜想成月亮的、氧气的
必须把你 想成未来的分泌物

但别去想 在记忆的剧痛中
那个向你咆哮的 烂掉的
你不愿称呼的人

因为那是从命运黑暗的尸骨上流下的
黏在人生指间的粘液和脓血

嗅吧，你能嗅到吗

也不必去想那个恐惧的人
在抛弃的红唇里说话
在背叛的明眸里……转开视线

想一想那个撞死在胸脯的岩石上的人
像一只毫无希望的凤凰
像一只滑进地狱的狂怒的凤凰

一座幸存奴隶们的忠诚的地狱

求存的儿童不能想起爱
不能熄灭耳光
从掐断的幼芽上长出世界

## Fake Smile

Each day the light of rebirth,
The agony of this ulcerous existence

The excruciated heart held up
For the mercy of wings to nurse:
I'm rotting away!

Imagine the night into summer,
The summer moonlit, fresh
Imagine you secreted by the future,

Without reviving, in the acute memory of pain
You don't want to mention
The decomposed shout of that man

That was slime, that was pus, stuck between fingers,
Oozing from fate's dark carcass

Can you smell it?

No need to recall the frightened one,
Lips red with desertion,
Shy of betrayal's glamorous gaze

Imagine instead the one dashed dead against the rock
Of a human chest, a desperate phoenix,
The furious slide into hell

Hell for the living loyal slaves

Struggling to live, children conjure love,
Cannot soften their slapped faces,
Worlds sprouting out of nipped buds

不能消化吗？不能呕出吗？
当夏夜裹着我们的氧气……
当月光……当白花……没有母亲
没有。

所以，必须不去想孩子
因为我已经枯萎了
在无望的、洗脑的粘液中
她的奴隶也能指使我强作笑颜

Can they be digested? Vomited?
Summer nights wrapped in our breath,
Moonlight . . . white flowers . . . no mothers there.

I will not think of children,
I'm already withered.
In this slime of amnesia
Only slaves can force a smile.

5 Poems by Tong Wei

*Translated by Stephen Haven and Li Yongyi*

**小木偶**

谁伸入她——
五指操纵她的心灵
她刚要诉说
孤儿般漂泊的身影
停息
在花朵的指尖

伸入天空的树木
顶着鹿角疾驰
天空的镜子碎了

手像树上的毛虫
掉进草地
她摇曳月光的绳子
黑色的小心脏，奔向月亮
在银匣子里震响

我在缝——
在她早已摔破的哭泣中
缝时间的面具
在她笑意昂然的颧骨上
我把伤口——
移植到早晨的镜里

小木偶，小木偶
长着不再惊呼的嘴
光的睫毛
从灰暗的肩膀
一圈圈剥落
一双手交叉、重叠
滑入我骨纹消逝的头颅
已缝合成
非人的器官

## LITTLE PUPPET

Whose penetrating fingers
Manipulate her little heart?
She speaks of an orphaned
Homunculus perched
On the tip of a flower

Trees stretching into the sky
Race past, crowned with antlers
The blue mirror breaks

Hands like caterpillars from trees
Dangling down to the grass
She pulls at the string of light,
That little black heart craving for the moon,
Rattling in the silver box

I'm sewing—
In her broken sobs
Sewing a mask of time
Onto her smiling cheekbones
I'm transplanting the wound
Into the mirror of morning

Little puppet, little puppet,
Your mouth no longer cries
For surprise, eyelashes of light
Peel off
Your gloomy shoulders,
Your crossed, overlapped hands
Sliding into my seamless skull
Sewn into an inhuman thing

**遗产**

散乱的灰发
披在檐架上
一圈蜂群飞向瓦房
那里撑着毒伞
看护白骨的显露
灵车颠簸于青草
死亡穿越白色马路
与行人再次面晤

我在一个夏夜陪伴
听她的呼吸进入瓦斯突破的隧道
窒息致使青春魅力再现
她把她的挣扎交给我
让我抖落记忆如尘土

突然,和她的面容撞个满怀
……我的外祖母,一只候鸟
正降落在梦魇的支架上
她重新穿戴她的皮肤如此光彩
她穿过田野疯狂跳舞
她转向我——
操纵鸟的语言

## Inheritance

Disheveled gray hair
Hangs on the eaves of the house
A swarm of bees flies to the tiled frame
There, a poisoned umbrella
Guards exposed bones
The hearse bumps on the grass,
Death crosses the white road
Meets again each passerby

On a summer night, I sat by her bed,
By the thin tunnel of her breath
Suffocation squeezed the charmed youth back
When she entrusted her struggle to me
I shook off dust-like memories

My grandmother, bird of passage,
Alights on the nightmare's frame,
Sudden flash of her face
Puts on her brilliant skin again
She dances wildly across the fields,
Heads for me, controlling
The birds and everything they are saying

**小木马**

它睁着圆圆的眼睛望着窗外
只有阳光咬住树叶的声音
叶子像风的耳朵飘在地上
孩子蒙住它晕眩的脸
像被梦游人驮着奔跑
"梦真好,别让我停下来"

它从木质的肌肉里
挤出残废的微笑
被孩子夹住的笑声
"嗒嗒嗒"走着,从它的黑暗里
一张衰老的面容站起身
"不,不是这样"

## The Wooden Horse

Its pearly eyes gaze through the window
It only hears the toothed sunlight grind leaves
They drift to the ground like the wind's ears
Dizzy, blindfolded by children,
The horse swirls around, carried by a somnambulist
"If this is dreaming, don't let me stop"

From its wooden muscles
Oozes a crooked smile,
Laughter choked by children
Time tips out of its darkness
Then it surfaces, the shriveled face:
"No, no, it's not like this"

Does not open its dumb mouth

**活着，在这个城市**

此时是午夜
一个匆忙的旅行者
怎么能理解你沉睡的
冬天，已经来临；
但你细心，想说些
安慰世界的话语
那个擦肩而去的生命
它把你带走
再也无需送回
那里，黎明
伏在膝盖骨制成的铲车上
驶入风雪的家园。
我听见交谈声
继续在周围传播
听见不真实的消息
从固执的天边闪现
生为女人，也许要像只鸟儿
以羽毛编制精致的披肩
但如果你爱上了
一个人，被捕获在
一棵灿烂冬树的热望
她苦味的针叶枝
刺痛生长的句子
绿色，绿色……更绿的苍茫
当这个世界的情感患病了
吸尽一缕微光
散步着相互致意的时间
……

## Living This City

It's midnight
How can the rushed traveler
Understand the advent
Of sleeping winter?
But you, being considerate, want to say
A few words to comfort the world,
That life churned by
Took you away, never
Brought you back
There dawn, prostrate
On a forklift made of knees,
Drives into the home of wind, snow
I hear voices
Murmuring around,
News, never verified,
Flashes in an obstinate sky
A woman imitates a bird,
Weaving a feathered shawl
But if you fall in love
You will be caught by the desire
Of a winter-lit tree
Her coniferous twigs
Needle your growing poems,
Green, green, confusion of an evergreen
When the world contracts a disease
Time chunks breathe in dim light
Walk together, greeting each other
    ...

她的没有金盏花的视野开阔。
谁留在这里,那里?
谁被声音和眼睛挽留
谁健康地活在某个角落
多遗憾——北极似的房间
雪莲堆积着火焰
没有人能砍去和得到
只是逼迫
相信不再有
过去的冬天还活着;
一位往日的司炉工
挥舞,铁铲上闪耀勇气
一场毕生的锻炼
坐在危险的境地
火映照,雅致
而强烈的诱惑;
她情愿输给你们
取走头巾,手套还有荣誉
让你们愉快地下个赌注吧
死亡要占领它自己的地区
痛苦——只是预约的时间

She does not have the marigold's eye . . .
Who, kept back by voices and visions,
Lives in some healthy nook?
What a shame—in that icy room
Saussurea flames, dances
Who can gain by chopping away?
Who can believe
The still-living past winters?
An old fireman
Wields his shovel, courage,
Forging a lifetime,
Sits in that perilous space
Reddened by the tongues of fire,
Elegant, seductive
She is ready to yield to you
Take away the gloves, her scarfed honor
Lay a wager to your heart's content
Death will occupy its territory,
Suffering, the only rendezvous

## 贝壳

海浪当你像一排绵羊胆怯地站立起
在搭乘海船的瞬间
又像剃光了卷发的羔羊潜返回海底

海里有沙,沙里有贝壳
它们张开了眼
与我一同观赏

每一回,与贝壳分享
每一夜,浸湿的月光
极薄的,陡峭的,贴在冰冷的脸颊

而一只抛入海水的瓶子
没有,没有人知道它想去哪里
四处漂流却隔绝着什么

在岸上……幻觉……有时候
游向再度晕眩的海
那贝壳就像一颗心胆怯地站立起

当它离去的瞬间,我看见
海贝就像那等待剖光的作品
发出绝望的乞求:

"将我潜返至海底
并且——带上一颗濒死的
心,那共有的凹陷——要共诉。"

## Shells

Riding on waves, a row of timid sheep
When they swirl you sink back
To the seafloor, lambs shorn

Sand in the sea, shells in the sand,
They open their eyes
Gazing at the world with me

Time spent with them
Every night, the dripping moonbeams,
Thin, steep, cling to the cold faces

When a bottle is cast into the sea
No one knows where it intends to go,
Drifting freely, in its solitude

Thrown on the shore, my illusions
Swim again to the watery vertigo
A shell, one timid heart, rises to meet them

Washed back, what a wonder
Is sealed in darkness again
It pleads in desperation:

"Send me back to the seafloor
With my dead heart—the shared cave
Will utter our common sorrow."

4 Poems by Wang Jiaxin

*Translated by Stephen Haven and Jin Zhong*

**铁**

沉甸甸的,黑,比夜还黑
比一个暴君还要镇定。
我看到黑暗中的炼铁厂,火
烧红了一个世纪
在酷夏呼啸而来,铁的力量
压倒一切。
铁,岩石之父,这是
来自男人性格中的某种东西
黑暗
而盲目:它在那里
在呈现的言词,与更广大的
虚无之间,它是一个否定
但比肯定还要
肯定:它是铁,是坚定无言
不可破灭的
铁。

## IRON

Heavy, dark, darker than night
Cooler than the mind of a tyrant
I see an ironworks in the dark, the fire
Tormenting a whole century.
Whizzing near in June, the force of iron
Overwhelms everything.
Iron, the father of rock, it is
Something from the nature of man,
Dark
And blind: It is there
Between the words presented and the greater
Nothingness. It is a negation
Yet it is more affirmative
Than affirmation: It is iron. It is the indomitable
Indisputable, and indestructible
Iron.

**火车站**

车站,这废弃的
被出让给空旷的,仍留着一缕
火车远去的气息
车轮移动,铁轨渐渐生锈

但是死亡曾在这儿碰撞
生命太渴望了,以至于一列车厢
与另一列之间
在呼喊一场剧烈的枪战

这就如同一个时代,动词们
相继开走,它卸下的名词
一堆堆生锈,而形容词
是在铁轨间疯长的野草……

## Train Station

This station, abandoned,
Given up to emptiness
Still possesses some slight sounds
Of the departing train
The wheels moved away, the rails rusted slowly

Death collided here
Life was so thirsty that each car
Challenged the others fiercely
To a constant gunfire...

One after the other, the verbs of this era
Vanished, the nouns were unloaded from it
Heap after rusty heap, and the adjectives—
Weeds along the rails rampantly growing

**楼梯**
北京和平门旧居

每当我
踏上这危险的楼梯,以缓慢的步子
盘旋,到达
并点亮灯

如同模仿一种仪式,再次回来
依然被这楼梯
在黑暗中领着

敲门
仿佛有谁正等着我
也许,在屋子里的
是一个多年前的自己
会把黑暗打开

## STAIRCASE
*written in my old home at the Gate of Peace*

Every time I spiral up
The dangerous stairs,
With slow steps
I reach the door
Turn on the light

Like some worn ceremony
I come back to these stairs
Again they lead me up
Through darkness
I do not take out my key
Instead, I raise my hand to knock
As if somebody were waiting for me

Maybe, inside the apartment
My old self many years ago
Will open the darkness

**转变**

季节在一夜间
彻底转变
你还没有来得及准备
风已扑面而来
风已冷得使人迈不出院子
你回转身来,天空
在风的鼓荡下
出奇地发蓝

你一下子就老了
衰竭,面目全非
在落叶的打旋中步履艰难
仅仅一个狂风之夜
身体里的木桶已是那样的空
一走动
就晃荡出声音

而风仍不息地从这个季节穿过
风鼓荡着白云
风使天空更高、更远
风一刻不停地运送着什么
风在瓦缝里,在听不见的任何地方
吹着,是那样急迫

剩下的日子已经不多了
落叶纷飞
风中树的声音
从远方溅起的人声、车辆声
都朝着一个方向

## Change

The season has completely changed
Overnight
Before you have time to protect yourself
The wind sears your face
The wind so cold you can't walk out of your yard
You turn back, the sky
Swept by the wind
Reveals its extraordinary hue

You go suddenly septuagenarian
Exhausted, distorted beyond recognition
You walk with difficulty in whirlpools
Of falling leaves
After just one night of violent wind
The wooden bucket in your body empties
If you move
You will hear it rocking

The wind-pierced, cloud-swept season
Heightens the remote sky
Constantly transporting something
The wind presses the chinks between the tiles
Into cries
Presses into places you cannot hear

The days still remaining are numbered
The dead leaves scattering about
The sound of trees in the wind
The sounds of people and their stirred vehicles
In the distance, everything heading
In the same direction

如此逼人
风已彻底吹进你的骨头缝里
仅仅一个晚上
一切全变了
这不仅使你暗自惊心
把自己稳住,是到了在风中坚持
或彻底放弃的时候了

Hurry up!
The wind blown completely into your joints
Just one night everything has changed
It suddenly sobers you up:
It is time to keep going in the wind
Or to give up everything

A Poem by Li Yongyi

*Translated by the Author*

## 天命

（一）以色列

仇恨你成了一门艺术，一种哲学
一套千年不断的生产线：谣言
演说，专著，节日的戏剧表演
十字架，火刑台，毒气室，坑穴

比雅典和罗马更古老，但你却
任人践踏，仿佛布满霉斑的馒头
无论敌我，战争总是你的诅咒
他们握手言欢，你仍一汪血泊

你贡献了耶稣，世界却只记得
犹大，你创造思想、宗教和科技
世界却还给你废墟、流浪和隔离
你一忍再忍，世界却一错再错

甚至复国都几乎让你再次丧国
上帝拣选了你，却拒绝拣选和平
漩涡的中心，永恒的耶路撒冷
在梦中追问当初蜜和奶的承诺


（二）德意志

闪电般你攻陷了文学，狂飙中
将哲学纳入版图，铁血的车间
铸造新的帝国，工业的峰巅
你的笑容璀璨。文明人的瞳孔

被惊愕点燃，硫磺火从嘴唇里
倾巢而出：下贱的普鲁士，匈奴
野蛮的德国鬼，邪恶的敌基督……
围攻梦想，蔑视的旗遮天蔽日

## Destinies

I. Israel

This hatred of you, an art, a philosophy
A ghastly perennial assembly line: gossip,
Oratory, monographs, festival shows,
Crosses, gyres, gas chambers, pits.

For you, older than Athens and Rome,
Trampled, crushed like moldy bread,
War, a stabbed curse, whoever fights.
In peace, you're still steeped in gore.

Jesus your gift, Judas your heritage.
Ideas, beliefs, inventions you give;
Debris, ghettos you get in return.
You endure, endure; they err and err.

Restored, your country almost lost
Again. God chose you, but not peace.
In fire eternal Jerusalem seeks
That first promise of honey and milk.

II. Germany

You blitzed literature, took philosophy
In a whirlwind. Casts of iron and blood
Forged a new empire, your smile lit up
Summits of industry. Civilized eyes

Astounded, ablaze, sulfurous flames
Burst out their lips: Prussians, Huns,
Barbaric Boche, the Anti-Christ....
Besieging your dreams, flags darkened the sun.

坚定的逻辑,和更坚定的偏见
路德挑衅教皇,更挑衅犹太族
康德的星空按肤色排列着光谱
黑格尔把汉语埋入史前的悬棺

一战你对抗欧洲,二战你对抗
整个世界,千万具青春的躯体
被运转不息的观念碾压成血泥
直到奥斯威辛休克了你的思想

日尔曼先祖的基因停止了喧嚣
柏林墙隔开了劫灰之前的年月
纳粹未曾焚尽的那些画卷和书页
在莱茵河的暮色中无言地飘……


(三)美利坚

精神的国土,被以色列和罗马
一分为二:国会山、鹰徽和军队
把英语变成了拉丁,而你的约柜
藏在旧欧洲和例外论的言辞下

新大陆和未来,如同成型的过去
不可更改,为了加尔文的上帝
你在种植园、交易所和淘金地
追逐财富、救赎和美国梦的喜剧

女巫的骨灰中,你学会政教分离
英王的税,启示了宪法的条文
程序正义赶走了东部的印第安人
奴隶的自由为工业创造了价值

感动于自己的道德,你却屡番
尴尬于利益,欢迎一切苦难者
你却时常成了苦难的不可解结
世界需要你,只因没更好的法官?

Your hard logic stood and harder prejudice.
Luther provoked Pope, cursed the Jews.
Kant's stars ordered to the colors of the skin,
Hegel buried Chinese in pre-historic gloom.

In World War I you fought Europe, and in II
You fought the world. Millions of young bodies
Bulldozed into pulp by an ever-churning Idea
Until Auschwitz paralyzed your mind.

The genes of your Germanic fathers ebbed.
The Berlin walls excluded the centuries
Before the mayhem, cinders of volumes
Burned by the Nazis blowing above the Rhine.

III. USA

Spiritual territory divided by Israel and Rome,
Capitol, the eagle and the military
Turned English into Latin, your ark of covenant
Lurking in "Old Europe" and exceptionalism

The future of the New World, like the formed past,
Stands unalterable. To glorify a Calvinist God
In plantations, stock exchanges, gold valleys,
You pursue wealth, salvation, the American comedy.

Witch ashes taught you to sever law from religion,
Taxes from the Crown inspired your Constitution,
Procedural justice drove Indians West,
And slaves' liberty brought new value to industry.

Moved by your own virtue, embarrassed
At your profit, you embrace all who suffered,
Yourself an aporia of suffering.
The world needs you in the absence of a better judge?

（四）俄罗斯

你的广袤令敌人垂涎，继而绝望
一切牺牲都可忍受，村庄焚灭
牛羊屠尽，死者遍地堆积如草芥
生者让生理学崩溃，心理学投降

你的苦难深沉如贝加尔湖，力量
隐秘如西伯利亚虎，雄浑的山水
隔绝了交通，执拗的枯骨与鬼魅
却在彼得堡的泥沼里学会合唱

金帐国的欺凌，第三罗马的梦想
希腊式的字母，拜占庭的血脉
你渴慕自由，却时常拥抱独裁
帝国才是你真正的图腾和信仰

但你永远高于浅薄的政治，思想
让你成为巨人，你有诚实的圣哲
坚忍的流放犯和灵魂的拷问者
在漫长的冬天为世界积攒食粮


（五）迦太基

欧罗巴的后代，欧洲的祖先
你也曾主宰地中海的阴晴
现在，你只是大漠的一缕烟
一面神话和历史中的妖镜

多情的女王，真的曾经爱上
仓皇的埃涅阿斯？抑或是
拉丁语凯旋后的中年臆想
为血湖添上些柔靡的涟漪

阴郁的汉尼拔，徒然被毒誓
禁锢了一生，迷惑的大象
在阿尔卑斯的雪中可曾问你
如果没有罗马，你去何方？

IV. Russia

Your sheer size imbues enemies with desire, despair.
No costs insufferable to you, villages destroyed,
Livestock wiped out, lands blanketed with corpses,
Survivors shame physical and psychological laws.

Deep as Lake Baikal your pain, your power secretive
As a Siberian tiger. Colossal mountains and rivers
Impede communications, but bone and ghosts, obstinate,
Learned to sing in chorus in Petersburg's swamps.

Bullied by Mongols, you yearned to be Third Rome,
Adopting a Greek-styled alphabet and Byzantium blood.
Thirsting for freedom, you more often embraced despotism,
Empire being your true totem and tenet.

Yet you always stand higher than politics, thoughts
Make you a giant. Locked securely away,
Your honest sages, enduring exiles and penitents,
Will store food for the world in endless winter.

V. Carthage

Europa's offspring, forefather of Europe,
You too used to control the Mediterranean waves,
But now a mere stroke of smoke in the desert,
A ghostly mirror in history and myth.

That amorous queen truly gave her heart
To a vagabond Aeneas? Or more likely
A middle-aged fantasy of triumphant Latin
Adds a veneer of decadence to a blood lake.

Gloomy Hannibal, bound in vain by an oath
To a life of killing. Did bewildered elephants,
Half-buried in Alpine snow, ask him where
He would go if there had been no Rome?

深陷敌阵的孤军,几乎灭掉
整个民族,坎奈的尸山下
隆起一个帝国,他的燃烧
将熔尽另一个文明的骨架


(六)斯巴达

不歌咏雅典,因你的鬼魂
比宿敌的记忆更强大,鸡鸣
不能惊吓,晓色不能隐沦
无声的咒语囚禁意志的清明

三百勇士的壮美,动魄惊心
每位死者都曾是幸存的婴孩
城邦的共产,陌生的双亲
军营灌注他们,对仇恨的爱

夜幕下,无人窥见的身影
留下一具奴隶愕然的尸体
翌日,长老们严肃的神情
告诫他,成人礼仅仅是开始

内战的废墟迎来了马其顿
但你从未朽烂,甚至柏拉图
都梦想在他的天国旧梦重温
甚至自由者都迷恋你的肃穆

A lonely army, wrapped by its enemy, nearly
Annihilated a nation. Under the carnal mountain
Erupted an empire, flames would consume
The skeleton of its rivaling civilization.

VI. SPARTA

I won't sing Athens, your ghost more powerful
Than the memory of that eternal enemy,
Undeterred by the rooster, unsinkable by dawn,
Silent spell confining any sober mind.

The beauty of the three hundred startles,
Each dead a child that had survived,
Property of the polis, parents unknown,
Taught to love hate in a soldiers' camp.

In the dark, an unseen shadow left behind
The body of a surprised slave.
Next morning, the elders warned him,
Solemnly, of the recurring initiation.

Ruins after the civil war ushered in
Macedonia, but you've never gone rotten.
Even Plato dreams of you in his heaven,
Even liberals enthrall to your order.

7 Poems by Yu Nu

*Translated by Stephen Haven and Li Yongyi*

**布道者**

我四处游走,飘忽于精神之上
经历石头和花朵。一件事物
与一件事物,一双手
和另一双手,它们都是我沟通的目的

我巧舌如簧
钻营在事件与事件的中心

我大气一样弥漫,不可抵御
集合起云
和涣散的人心
无孔不入。带着干粮,水
一身清凉的火焰

在富有质感的游说中,我被他们悄悄抽象
出神入化  亲近我宗教的面颊
以异端的嘴巴

老谋深算,我要的就是这些外衣
剥开它们
或者就被它们封闭

## The Preacher

I wander around, floating above the spiritual,
Living stones and flowers. One thing
And another, one hand, another hand,
All stretch at the end of my communion.

Drilling with a cunning tongue
I maneuver at the center of things.

Ubiquitous as air, irresistible,
I gather clouds,
Divided hearts,
Reaching every nook with my food, water,
Flames refreshingly cool.

My conviction abstracts them
Into a deity I lobby.
They approach my devout cheeks
Heresy in their mouths.

I calculate, I crave these trappings:
Either I unravel them
Or they enclose me.

**守夜人**

钟敲十二下,当,当
我在蚊帐里捕捉一只苍蝇
我不用双手
过程简单极了
我用理解和一声咒骂
我说:苍蝇,我说:血
我说:十二点三十分我取消你
然后我像一滴药水
滴进睡眠
钟敲十三下,当
苍蝇的嗡鸣,一对大耳环
仍在我的耳朵上晃来荡去

## The Watchman

The clock chimed twelve
I was hunting down a fly in my mosquito net
Without using a hand
I was doing it extra simple:
Through empathy and a curse
I said: fly, I said: blood
I said: I cancel you out at twelve thirty
Then I dripped into sleep
Like the seep of some elixir
The clock chimed thirteen,
The buzz of the fly, enormous rings
Still dangling from my ears

**环境**

苍蝇在盒子里,
磁带上的嗡嗡声。

缠着绷带的手表,
冰块里的嘀嗒声。

抽屉里一双烂梨,
木头的呼吸声。

用化名去死,
找不到尸体。

将这一切盖上盖子。

## Circumstance

This fly in the box
Buzzing on a tape.

This bandaged watch
Clicking in ice blocks.

Couple of rotten pears
Breathing of wood.

Die with an alias
No corpse found.

Hide all this under a lid.

**剧情**

你在干什么
我在守卫疯人院

你在干什么
我在守卫疯人院

你在干什么
我在守卫疯人院

我写诗，拔草，焚尸
数星星，化装，流泪

## The Action

What are you doing
I'm guarding the madhouse

What are you doing
I'm guarding the madhouse

What are you doing
I'm guarding the madhouse

I write poems, pull up weeds, burn bodies,
Count stars, dress, weep

**抑郁**

在静物里慢慢弯曲
在静物里
慢慢弯曲

在
静物里

慢慢,弯曲:汤汁里的火苗
隆冬的猫爪
一张弓在身体里
咔嚓一声折断

## Depression

Bending slowly in still life,
Bending slowly
Still in life,
Slowly bending in

Life still: flames in broth,
Cat claws in deep winter,
A bow inside the body
Snaps in half

**有水的瓶子**

瓶子被绳子捆着,
声音出不来。

感官里的昆虫团团转。
一只钩子在生长。

被吃掉的曲线。
原汁原味的鱼。

一句话和一个固体。
他坐在概念中,
张口一个死结。

## Bottle with Water

Strapped up by a cord
The bottle gives no sound.

Insects whine and circle.
A hook grows.

A curved line eaten up.
A fish stewed in its own juices.

Sentences and solids.
He sits in an idea,
Dead knot in an open mouth.

## 目睹

早晨的空气被抽掉了,大麻造成的不愉快
使他和她互相取代。远处,一个玩球的少年
不见了,河面上漂着他的帽子,软组织像
割断的水藻一样,无人过问。那是７６年
我一个人住在花园里,才１０岁,夜里
我害怕极了(你听见过夜间花开的
声音吗?),同时我看见
一条鱼,在福尔马林里游来游去
那一刻我有着瓶子一样的预感:他和她
眼睛和躯干, 两个盲人的机械装置
将在花园里被拆散,植物的苦闷
都是这样,心里明白,却说不出口
直到一朵花出现,或卖血为生的妇人
在血中隐匿,躲在那里,永不露面
像我二十年后所做的,用雨水说话
描写那一年的十一月,用调匀的颜色
说,用伸缩着的阴影说。在惊呆的月光下
他站着,二十年了,她呼吸的灰尘
还围绕着他,她的脸
被一把锁锁着,看不清,也没有留下
一张照片,从那时起,我就只相信感官
她是鸟走后留下的尸体,是一张纸上
残存的理性之肉
随风飘着,纯属捏造。现在我回来了
那个少年却没有回来,花园里
找不到他的骨骸。两个人
埋伏在一个人的身上,多少年不发一语
他们想干什么?由此我肯定
我是一只混蛋月亮,把什么都看在眼里
在草丛中,在堆放着旧轮胎的小径上

## The Eyewitness

Morning air pumped off, cannabis-induced despondency
Replaced him and her. Far away, his ball-playing days,
His cap floating on the river, his soft tissues
Like severed seaweeds. This happened in 1976.
I was living alone in the garden, barely ten, frightened
At night, trembling. Have you ever heard a flower
Bloom? I saw
A fish shuttling in formaldehyde.
Then I had the inkling of being bottled: He and she,
Eyes and bodies, gadgets of two blind beings,
Torn to nothing. The sorrow of flora:
They understand, they can't speak—
A blossom emerges, a woman living by selling her blood
Hidden in blood, cowering, never seen again,
Just what I did these years later, uttered in rain
The November of that year, those well-tuned colors,
Shadows that shrink and expand. Under a stunned moon,
He stands, these decades later, the dust she breathed
Cornering him still, her face
Locked, not a single picture left.
Ever since then, I've trusted my senses only,
Her corpse deserted by birds, the flesh of all reason
Swinging on a sheet of paper,
That fiction surviving in the wind. Now I'm back
In that absent adolescence. No bones of his
Found in the garden. Two people
Buried speechless in one body.
Therefore I'm sure
I'm the scoundrel moon, seeing everything
In the grass, these many years, old tires in the path.

6 Poems by Zheng Min

*Translated by Stephen Haven and Li Yongyi*

**发生在四月昏暗的黄昏**

从玻璃窗,紧闭的,渗透进来
一片乌云,在房间里,天花板下流动
树叶像雨落下,淅淅漓漓
埋葬我的肉体,和它的没有熄灭的火焰
一只洁白的鸽子从尸体里飞出
它在高空望着残缺了的丑恶的墙
它飞行了几千里,落下在
菩提树下
饥渴地想到:有没有一家屋顶
一处广场,一个教堂的尖顶,能接受
漂流的雨云。

一个儿童伸出鲜嫩的手掌
让它啄食玉米粒
它想着那埋在落叶下的尸体。

## April Dusk

Through the window, clam-tight, oozes
A dark cloud, flowing beneath the ceiling.
Leaves rain down, drizzling,
Burying my body, the flames not yet dead.
A snow-white dove flies out among corpses,
Looking down, midair, at the ruin of ugly walls.
After traveling thousands of miles, it lands
In the shade of a bodhi tree,
Hungry, thirsty, musing: which roof,
Which square, which church steeple, can take in
A wandering rain-cloud?

A child reaches out his soft palm
Feeding it corn,
These leaf-covered bodies.

**海底的石像**

在空寂的屋里
天花板下流动
晚霞、金色夕阳
喷出缆车和游客
猛瞥见镜中的人像
无数几何形的头部
从深海处被打捞出
还带着古时
偶然留下的神态。
火山已经熄灭。

## Stone Statues on the Seafloor

In the still, empty room,
The setting sun's gold, the clouds' afterglow,
Ripple under the ceiling,
Spitting out cable-cars and tourists.
Statues, suddenly glimpsed in the mirror,
Countless geometrical skulls
Fished from the deep sea,
Still keep their expressions
Caught off guard, ancient times.
These extinct volcanoes.

**《戴项链的女人》**
(意画家莫迪里阿尼一九一七年作)

火红的头发
一朵燃烧着的大丽花
长在黑色的土地上
那黑丝绒长袍裹着
秋天的身体,下溜的
半露的肩,微胖的臂膀
和那连接着思维和躯体的
细长、棕色的脖子
腰仍在留连着少女的年月。

深隽的一双黑眸子
醒悟了的意识又被
世纪初西方的迷惘催眠
怔怔地半垂着的视线
然而眼睑却没有松弛
时间的脱节引起了肌理的失调。

仿佛感到法国梧桐的大叶子
在变硬,
太阳是午夜后的舞会
大丽花和月季
这不知疲倦的舞伴还在
拼命地唱、跳和呼喊
然而夏天终于是被摔弃的火箭
项链断断续续地挂在胸前
珠子、希望、眼泪、多情的凝视
都从这胸前滴下
当黑色的丝绒长袍裹住
秋天的身体,而大丽花仍在
燃烧、火红的头发。

从粉红色的婴儿走向
长着鹰爪样关节的风湿老年
她正瞧着一扇半开的时间的门
从那里通向
晚霞消逝后冷静的晚空。

### Modigliani's Woman with Red Hair

The fire-red hair,
A burning dahlia,
Roots in black soil.
That black velvet gown wraps
An autumnal body, its declining
Shoulder, half-revealed plumpish arm,
Its slim brown neck
Connecting thoughts and torso,
The waist lingering in girlhood.

Black eyes barely awakened,
Hypnotized again
Confused by the Western début-de-siècle.
A downward locked-in glance,
No sleep in those young eyes,
Dislocated time. What erupts in that complexion?

She seems to feel the broad leaves of plane trees
Hardening.
The sun, an after-midnight ball,
Dahlias and roses,
Tireless dancers, singing,
Shouting like crazy.
Summer abandoned like a spent rocket:
The necklace hangs on her chest,
Beads, hopes, tears, wistful gazes,
Dripping down.
The black velvet gown drapes
Her autumnal body, that dahlia,
Her red hair, burns on.

Traveling from her pink infancy
To the eagle-clawed arthritis
She stares at time's half-opened door
Leading to the evening sky,
Cold, quiet, vanishing in the afterglow.

**穿过波士顿雪郊**

雪,
挤进来
又被风
扫出去
这样渴望遮住
　穿过冬林的灰蛇长路,
它的铅色的脸,
焦虑的车擦过
　雾中的冬林
　　　它只剩下
大张着的嘴
拧着的手臂
祈求的姿态
无声的呼喊
刺痛耳朵
这些沉寂的
　　　黑色的树林

我们谈到童年
雪地上的痕迹
迤逦追随
前面的轨迹,
加上我们的,
加上
我们后面的。
偶尔说几句话
今天的,以前的
这儿的,那儿的。

## Crossing Boston Suburbs in Snow

Snow
Squeezing in
Swept again
By the wind
So quickly veils
    The snake, gray road, its leaden face
In winter woods,
The anxious car rustles by
    Foggy trees
        Where we can see
Gaping mouths,
Twisted arms,
Silent cries
Drilling our ears.
So quiet
    These dark woods.

We talk of childhood.
Traces in the snow
As if in a line,
Tracks ahead,
Tracks left behind.
A few words now and then
About yesterday, here, there.

灰蛇蜿蜒进出树林
雪在挤进来
车在梦中开回家
对话浮出混沌的水面
又沉入海洋
鲸鱼的灰背的浮沉
童年，波士顿，雪
活过来的树林
更真实的部分
却没有发出声音。

The gray snake threads through,
Snow squeezes in,
In a dream, the car heads for home.
Words rise above water
Sink into the chaotic ocean.
The grey rhythm of the whale's back,
Childhood, Boston, snow.
The awakening woods
Utters never a sound.

**渴望：一只雄狮**

在我的身体里有一张张得大大的嘴
它像一只在吼叫的雄狮
它冲到大江的桥头
看着桥下的湍流
那静静滑过桥洞的轮船
它听见时代在吼叫
好像森林里象在吼叫
它回头看着我
又走回我身体的笼子里
那狮子的金毛像日光
那象的吼声像鼓鸣
开花样的活力回到我的体内
狮子带我去桥头
那里，我去赴一个约会

## Longing, a Lion

Inside my body there is a gaping mouth,
A lion roaring
Rushing to the end of the bridge
As a ship glides by
Looking down at the river's rush
It hears the clamor of the times
Like an elephant's trumpet in the forest,
Throws a backward glance at me
Into the cage of my body
The lion's golden hair dazzles like the sun,
The call of the elephant's drum
This charge blooms in me,
Lures me to the bridge edge

**每当我走过这条小径**

每当我走过这条小径
幽灵就缠住我的脚步
我全身战栗,不是因为寒冷
而是看到那灼热的目光
年轻的星辰不应如此迅速的冷却
你们那茂盛的黑发
难道已化成灰烬
那鲜红的嘴唇
难道已滴尽了血液
你们的肢体充满弹性
如今却已经随风飘散
没有骨灰,没有灵位
啊!上天赐给的生命
竟成一场狞笑的误会
即使有人的良心抽搐
谁又能将风雨摧落的苹果
重接上枝头,还给我们
那青春的嫩须,还给母亲们
那曾在腹中蠕动的胎儿?
今年这里的绿叶又已成荫
蔷薇疯狂地爬满篱墙
玫瑰的红,茉莉的白,
野花的娇黄和深紫
都照常来到
惟有你们的脚步声
只出现在黑黑的深夜
在想念你们的梦中

我怕走上这条小径
却又抵挡不住你们的召唤
从这里我曾走向疯狂了的你们
我的胸腔因此胀痛
现在血已流尽,只剩下
尸体上苍白的等待
只剩下等待,等待
将像黑暗中的蘑菇
悄悄的生长。

## Ghost Path, 1990

Every time I walk this path
You trip up my gait
I tremble, not from the ghost cold,
But from your heat
So young, so soon
The black lushness of your hair
Turned to cinder, dust,
Your scarlet lips
Drained of their last blood
And your taut bodies
Blown by winds,
No bones, no plaques for memory
Where is heaven?
The chance that sneered at you?
If conscience cramped again,
Who could lift fallen apples
Back to their green limbs? Oh mothers,
Oh babies rolling in the womb,
In the leaf-woven shade,
Blossoms sprawling on walls,
Roses, white jasmines,
Pale yellow, dark purple
What flower ever missed its rendezvous?
Your footfalls sound in the dark night,
Dream of those missing you

I'm afraid to take this walk
But your call is irresistible,
Swollen in my chest
Now, your blood-dry zeal,
Pallor of waiting death,
Mushrooms in the dark.

6 Poems by Yang Jian

*Translated by Stephen Haven and Li Yongyi*

**夕光**

小时候,我在大堤上奔跑的时候见过江水上
渐渐西沉的落日,
长大后我才知葬身于它
又有何妨?
葬身,这大概就是我幸福的源头了。

当然,灵魂也可以细腻地存在,
比如墙头上枯草丛中的一只古瓮,
灵魂靠瓮盖上的一眼小孔,
靠暮晚时分的一缕夕光,
存活下来。

## Twilight

When a child, from the river bank:
The sun a slow ember over water.
Grown up, my entombment in it
Will surely not hurt
The light well of my being.

Certainly I can live more delicately,
Say, in an old urn on the wall stump
Covered by dried grass,
A tiny eye in the lid of that container,
That thin beam of twilight, dusk.

**馈赠**

树叶没有经过任何抵抗就落下了,
风,

又把它吹起,
它也是没有任何抵抗地"沙沙"作响。

在它瘦小,干枯的身体上,
爱,似乎比它在树干上的时候还要强烈。

是的,我是不死的,
也一定是这些树叶所赠。

## A Gift

The leaf, not resisting, falls,
And when the wind

Spins it around again,
It rustles, without resisting.

In its tiny wizened body, love breathes
More passionately than when on the tree.

Yes, I will not die,
A gift from these leaves.

**两个人静静的坐着**

两个人静静地坐着
拥抱使他们像岸边的石块一样僵硬。
小鸟在树林里尖叫着,
使他们的心儿紧缩。
在有柳树的水边上,
他们有着多么可怜的相爱的念头!
他忽然记起昨晚梦见的白发,
他想,一辈子为吃忙,
为了等到晚上跟她睡在一起,
他有了哭泣的念头。
他困惑地望着湖水,
望着靠在肩上的女人。
他们的身边是一个刚刚学会用腿走路的小孩,
和一个已经不会用腿走路的老人。
有个孕妇去摘水边的野花,
她的身旁,站着两眼茫然的丈夫。

## This Couple in Silence

The two sit in total silence,
Their hug as rigid as the rocks on the bank.
The shriek of birds in the woods
Shivers their hearts.
Under the willows
What sorry ideas of love!
Suddenly, he recalls the gray hair he dreamed last night,
The price paid for sleeping with her after dark.
This impulse to weep, this utter confusion:
He looks at the lake,
At the woman on his shoulder.
Nearby a child, a toddler,
An old man who can no longer walk,
A pregnant woman picking flowers by the shore,
Her husband standing by, blank eyes gazing nowhere.

**古老**

我所有活不长远的念头在一间草屋里消散一空,
那儿的地面由泥巴所做。

柴火烧的大灶上,
煮着一锅白米饭。

两块豆腐在碗底,
烂掉的白菜盖在上面。

那臭烘烘又香喷喷的白菜似乎就是古老的中国,
我所有活不长远的念头在这又矛盾又统一的气味里消散一空。

## Antiquity

All my fast thoughts vanish in a thatch house
Where the floor is made of earth and mud.

Over the log fire in the huge stove
White rice steaming from a wok.

Deep in a bowl slices of tofu
Covered by some rotten Chinese cabbage.

This sweet stench of baicai, old as China,
Stews even my sunk thoughts.

**暮晚**

马儿在草棚里踢着树桩,
鱼儿在篮子里蹦跳,
狗儿在院子里吠叫,
他们是多么爱惜自己,
但这正是痛苦的根源,
像月亮一样清晰,
像江水一样奔流不止……

## Dusk

The pony kicks the stump in the stable,
The fish thrashes in the basket,
The dog barks in the yard,
How they love and cherish themselves,
The very source of pain,
The still pulse of the moon,
The ceaseless river. . . .

**1967年**

他们说：
"这把二胡的弦要扯断，
琴身要砸碎。"
我们就没有了琴声。

他们说：
"这棵大树要锯断，
主要是古树，全部要锯掉。"
我们就没有了阴凉。

他们说：
"这个石匠要除掉，
那个木匠也要除掉，要立即执行。"
我们就没有了好看的石桥，
我们就没有了好看的房子。

他们说：
"这些圣贤的书要烧掉，
这些文庙要毁掉，
这些出家人要赶回家。"
我们就没有了道德，
我们就没有了良知。

我生于崩溃的1967年，
我注定了要以毁灭的眼光来看待一切，
我生下来不久就生病了，
我注定了要以生病的眼光来看待一切。

看着你们都在死去，
我注定了不能死去，
我注定了要在废墟上开口说话，
我注定了要推开尘封的铁门。

## 1967

They said:
"Tear off the erhu strings,
Smash its body."
We ended up without music.

They said:
"Chop this big old tree
Down to the stump."
We ended up without shade.

They said:
"Kill this stonemason,
That carpenter, right now."
We ended up without bridges,
Without pretty houses.

They said:
"Burn the ancient books,
Demolish the Confucian shrines,
Send the monks home to their mothers."
We ended up without a moral sense,
We ended up without conscience.

I was born in 1967, an apocalyptic year,
Destined to look at things with a destructive eye,
Sick soon after I entered the world,
Destined to look at things as a morbid man.

Seeing that you all are dying
I'm given to a life that cannot die,
My word on the ruins, sealed in dust,
The iron gate shoved open.

## Acknowledgments

Collaborative translations from *Trees Grow Lively on Snowy Fields* appeared in the journals below. Collaborative translators are credited after each individual poem by Mo Fei, and for all other poets translators are recognized on the first page of each section. "Destinies" by Li Yongyi was translated solo by the author. Many thanks to the editors of the journals below, especially to John Hennessey, Arthur Vogelsang, Rachel Morgan, and Jeremy Schraffenberger, for publishing translations in their pages.

*American Poetry Review*
Duo Duo: "It Is," "Longevity," "One Story Contains All His Past," "The Window that Loves to Weep," "In England"

Mo Fei: "Orchard," "Instant," "Facing a Stone," "That Stone," "Falling Snow"

Wang Jiaxin: "Iron," "Train Station," "Staircase," "Change"

*Artful Dodge*
Mang Ke: "City," "In the Street," One Night Stand," "Close Your Eyes," "Spring"

Gu Cheng: "Early Summer," "Sunset," "Partners," "The Enemy in Defensive Positions," "The Poet's Tragedy," "The Truth of It."

*Consequence Magazine*
Mang Ke: "Seashore*Seawind*Ship"

Gu Cheng: "Note to an Old Friend"

*The Common*
Yang Jian: "1967," "This Couple in Silence," "A Gift," "Antiquity"

Mo Fei: "Booming, Spring Shoves Open the Door," "The Man Trapped in the Room," "Silence, Just Dust on the Surface," "Hidden Grains Glisten in Winter," "Coins Tossed in All Directions"

Zheng Min: "Longing, a Lion," "Ghost Path, 1990," "Crossing Boston Suburbs in Snow," "Modigliani's Woman with Red Hair," "Stone Statues on the Seafloor"

Tang Danhong: "You Might Have Been My Brother," "Bent Morning," "Fake Smile"

Li Yongyi: "Destinies"

Yu Nu: "The Eyewitness," "The Preacher," "The Watchman," "Circumstance," "The Action," "Depression," "Bottle with Water"

*Manoa: Republic of Apples, Democracy of Oranges: New Eco-Poetry from China and the U.S.*
Yang Jian: "Dusk," "A Gift," "Twilight."

*North American Review*
Lan Lan: "Let Me Accept This Life," "Loss"

Yang Jian: "Twilight," "Dusk"

Mo Fei: "Trees Grow Lively on Snowy Fields," "Where Youth Is Not, You Begin"

*Poetry Miscellany*
Mang Ke: "People Age Even After Death," "You Dead Day," "Vineyard"

Gu Cheng: "Don't Take a Walk There," "Elegy"

*Two Lines*
Tong Wei: "Little Puppet," "The Wooden Horse"

Gu Cheng: "Cremation"

*World Literature Today*
Lan Lan: "The Gecko," "The World with You," "Only"

## Biographical Notes

Duo Duo won the prestigious Neustadt International Prize for Literature in 2010. Associated with the Chinese Misty School, he is one of the most important Chinese poets of our time. Born in 1951, he teaches at Hainan University, on Hainan Island, China. He has two collections of poems translated into English: *The Boy Who Catches Wasps: Selected Poetry of Duo Duo* (Zephyr Press, 2002), and *Looking Out from Death* (Bloomsbury 1990)

Gu Cheng was born in 1956. A prominent member of the Chinese Misty School, he lived in poverty and exile in New Zealand for the last years of his life. In 1993, in the midst of a quarrel over a lover, he murdered his wife and then committed suicide. Among the book-length English translations of his writing are *Sea of Dreams: The Selected Writings of Gu Cheng* (New Directions, 2005), and *Nameless Flowers: Selected Poems* (George Braziller, 2005).

Lan Lan is the best-selling author of nine poetry collections. She lives in Beijing and was born in Shandong Province in 1967. She has received many prizes for her poetry, including the Poetry & People Award, the Yulong Poetry Prize, and the "Best Ten Poets in China" Award. There are two book-length English translations of her work, *Nails* (Chinese University Press, 1990), and *Canyons in the Body* (Zephyr Press, 2014).

Li Yongyi is Professor of English at Chongqing University, in Chongqing, China. He was a 2012-2013 Fulbright Scholar in Residence at the University of Washington. He has translated the entire corpus of Roman poets Catullus, Horace, and Lucretius into Chinese, and his version of Horace won a Lu Xun Prize for Literary Translation (one of China's top prizes for literature) in 2018. He is also the author of three volumes of his own poems.

Mang Ke was co-founder (with Bei Dao) and Managing Editor of the journal *Jintian* (*Today*), first published in 1978 and central to the Chinese Misty School. Also an accomplished painter, and nationally recognized in China for his own poems and for his prominence in supporting the work of other poets, Mang Ke's poems have mainly appeared in China, with no book-length English translation of his writing. Born in 1951, he continues to live in Beijing.

Mo FEI was born in Beijing in 1960. He is a poet, photographer, gardener and naturalist. His poetry collection *Words and Things* was published in 1997, and his *Selected Poems of Mo Fei* appeared in 2011. He represents a mildly anti-establishment brand of contemporary Chinese poetry, neither nostalgic of native grassroots traditions nor overwhelmed by Western intellectual influences—the so-called Third Road.

TANG DANHONG was born in Chengdu in 1965. She is widely regarded as an avant-garde feminist poet and innovative filmmaker, drawing critical attention for her presentation of female sexuality and her culturally charged documentaries on Tibet. She was awarded the prestigious Liu Li'an Poetry Prize in 1995. Her most recent collection of poems appeared in 2012, *The X-ray, Sweet Nights*.

WANG JIAXIN is Professor of Literature and Director of the International Writing Center at the People's University in Beijing. He has published eight collections of poetry in Chinese, and many collections of literary essays. He was the 2007 Luce Poet-in-Residence at Colgate University and a 2013 fellow in the University of Iowa's International Writing Program. He is the primary Chinese translator of Paul Celan. Born in 1957, he lives in Beijing.

TONG WEI was born in Beijing in 1956. She was one of the leading female poets to win distinction in the 1980s when a new generation of authors began to work outside the influence of Misty School predecessors like Bei Dao, Gu Cheng, Mang Ke and Duo Duo. She made her unique contribution to Chinese poetry with snapshots of a secret world hovering between fairy tales and nightmares. She has published two collections of poems in China: *When the Horse Turns Its Head* (1988) and *Revenges on Dream-Addicts* (2012).

YANG JIAN was born in Anhui Province in 1967. He worked as a factory laborer for thirteen years. A practicing Buddhist and scholar of Chinese traditional culture, he began writing poetry during the mid-80s. He is the recipient of many national poetry awards, among them the prestigious Chinese Media Literature Award (2008). His books of poetry include *Dusk* (2003), *Old Bridge* (2007) and *Remorse* (2009).

YU NU was born in Anhui Province in 1966. He is the founder and soul of the Chinese Inexplicability School of Poetry. His work is characterized by minimalist, absurdist, and surrealist short poems. He is the author of *The Workman* and one other collection of poems.

ZHENG MIN was born in Fujian in 1920. A renowned poet, scholar and literary critic, she has published poetry since the early 1940s, eventually earning an M.A. in Literature from Brown University. She returned to China in 1955. A major influence on Chinese poetry written in the 1980s, she has published widely over the past thirty years, securing her iconic status in contemporary Chinese poetry.

## TRANSLATORS

STEPHEN HAVEN's most recent book of poems, *The Flight from Meaning*, was among eleven finalists for the International Beverly Prize for Literature. The collection will be published by London's Eyewear Publishing in 2021. Haven has published three previous collections of poetry, *The Last Sacred Place in North America* (2012, winner of the New American Press Poetry Prize), *Dust and Bread* (Turning Point, 2008, for which he was named Ohio Poet of the Year), and *The Long Silence of the Mohawk Carpet Smokestacks* (West End/University of New

Mexico Press, 2004). He is Professor of Literature and Creative Writing at Lesley University in Cambridge, MA.

JIN ZHONG's legal name is Jone Guo. He lives in Sabre Springs Valley, San Diego, California, often referred to in his poems and drawings as "Survivor's Village." He was born in Harbin, China, in 1962 and received an M.A. in English and American Literature at Beijing Foreign Studies University in 1989. Jin Zhong was exiled to the United States in 1991. His most recent book of poetry, *Morningside*, was published in China in 2014.

LI YONGYI: See author's note above.

WANG SHOUYI was formerly Dean of Foreign Languages and Professor of English at Heilongjiang University, in Harbin, China. As a Fulbright Professor from 1996-1997, he taught courses on the cross-cultural influences of Chinese and American poetry at Ashland University, in Ashland, Ohio. Later, he was a visiting professor at the University of Illinois, Springfield, and at the University of Houston. He has published twenty-one books (some co-authored), including two in the United States and a collection of his own poems, *Wish of Wind*. Two recent collections of collaborative translations (with the poet John Knoepfle) were published in China in 2018: *Snow on the River: Poems from the Tang and Song Dynasties of China* and *Voyage Home: Poems from the Yuan and Ming and Qing Dynasties of China* (Heilongjiang University Press). His co-translations from contemporary Chinese poems (with Stephen Haven) have appeared in various journals, including *Poetry Miscellany* (University of Tennessee), *Two Lines*, *Artful Dodge* and *Consequence Magazine*. He lives in Toronto, Canada, with his wife Suli.

Other Twleve Winters Press Titles for Lovers of Poetry

*The Waxen Poor*, J. D. Schraffenberger (poems)

*Starfish*, Pauline Uchmanowicz (poems)

*The Endless Unbegun*, Rachel Jamison Webster (poems & prose narratives)

*The Necessary Poetics of Atheism*, Martín Espada, Lauren Marie Schmidt & J. D. Schraffenberger (essays & poems)

*Extinguished & Extinct: An Anthology of Things That No Longer Exist*, edited by John McCarthy

Available through Amazon, Barnes & Noble, and independent bookstores. Visit twelvewinters.com.

www.ingramcontent.com/pod-product-compliance
Lightning Source LLC
Chambersburg PA
CBHW051647040426
42446CB00009B/1008